Flying High

Flying High

My Story: From AirAsia to QPR

TONY FERNANDES

PORTFOLIO
PENGUIN

PORTFOLIO PENGUIN

UK | USA | Canada | Ireland | Australia
India | New Zealand | South Africa

Portfolio Penguin is part of the Penguin Random House group of companies
whose addresses can be found at global.penguinrandomhouse.com.

First published 2017

001

Copyright © Tony Fernandes, 2017

The moral right of the author has been asserted

Set in 13.5/16 pt Garamond MT Std
Typeset by Jouve (UK), Milton Keynes
Printed in Great Britain by Clays Ltd, St Ives plc

A CIP catalogue record for this book is available from the British Library

HARDBACK ISBN: 978–0–241–00439–5
TRADE PAPERBACK ISBN: 978–0–241–00494–4

www.greenpenguin.co.uk

Penguin Random House is committed to a
sustainable future for our business, our readers
and our planet. This book is made from Forest
Stewardship Council® certified paper.

To the two most wonderful humans I helped create, Stephen and Stephanie. Continue being the most down to earth and caring people I know. Thanks for always being there for me.

Contents

Prologue: A Tuck Box of Dreams
Soundtrack: 'Dreams' by The Corrs

A few years ago a friend from my schooldays, Gerry Wig-field, rang out of the blue. Even at the other end of a long-distance phone line I could hear that he was excited.

'Tony, my mum's found something of yours.'

'What is it, Gerry?'

'Ah, that'd be telling. I'll get her to send it to you when you're next in London.'

I was staying in Kuala Lumpur for several months on business, so I admit that this conversation soon slipped my mind. A few days after I eventually arrived back in London and settled in my house in Chester Square, the doorbell rang. I padded to answer it dressed in my pyjamas, not really thinking about who or what might be waiting behind the door.

Standing there was our postman holding a parcel about three feet long by a foot high, wrapped in brown paper, with my name neatly printed on a white sticker. As he passed the box over I braced myself for something heavy, but it was surprisingly light. I put it down on a table in the hall, signed for the delivery and shut the door. For some reason the memory of Gerry's call came back to me and I ripped off the packaging.

A few seconds later, standing in a mess of brown paper, I started to well up. I was looking at a battered blue card-board chest with reinforced leather corners, brass locks and a leather strap at the end. It was my tuck box from my secondary school, Epsom College. I hadn't seen it for about thirty years.

On the lid of the box were three stickers: the badges of West Ham United, Qantas Airways and the Formula One team Williams.

I snapped the locks and lifted the lid. Inside were two C90 cassette tapes: Abba's *Arrival* and Steely Dan's *The Royal Scam*, as well as a packet of the dried noodles that my mum used to send me from Kuala Lumpur. The contents of the tuck box tipped me over the edge. I was a wreck. Memories of Mum, moving to England and my school life flooded over me.

The tuck box, inside and out, represented all the dreams I'd had when I was growing up: I loved sport, I loved music and I loved aeroplanes. What was so overwhelming for me in that moment was realizing that my childhood dreams had become my reality.

Since leaving Epsom, I had headed up a music business, partied with some of the biggest pop stars in the world and brought Malaysian and Asian bands to the global stage.

I had taken over an English football club and been carried on the shoulders of the players on the Wembley pitch after we won promotion.

I had stood on the starting grid at a Grand Prix with my own Formula One car.

I had acquired a tiny airline and transformed it into an international business carrying 70 million passengers a year.

Turning those dreams into reality – the journey from

putting stickers on my tuck box to opening the door to the postman some thirty years later – has been nerve-racking and heartbreaking at times, but packed full of excitement and joy. It also makes for a pretty unlikely and wildly unpredictable story.

But let's start at the beginning, where my early life and school career didn't show any signs of those dreams coming true.

1. About a Boy

Soundtrack: 'Georgia on My Mind' by Ray Charles

I pushed ten cents into the coin-operated binoculars and scanned the horizon. Nothing. I swivelled the binoculars round to point at the apron, studying the old turbo-prop planes, the Malaysia–Singapore Airlines' Fokker F27s and DC-3s, the Air Vietnam Vickers Viscounts and the tiny private Cessnas. I shifted again to look at the hangars beyond the runway, where planes were being worked on by the engineers. I turned back to look at the horizon. Still nothing.

'Relax, Anthony, we've got another hour before she lands,' said my dad.

We were standing on the viewing platform of Subang Airport, Kuala Lumpur. It was a humid day in July 1969, a few months after my fifth birthday. My dad, Stephen, and I were waiting for my mum to come home from another business trip.

It was the third time he had told me to relax. I nodded. The binocular lenses went dark, so I pushed another coin into the slot and turned my attention back to the apron. We stood side by side and silently looked out together.

Finally, the Fokker F27 came into view, a speck turning into the familiar shape, slowly growing in size and swooping in towards the runway. The moment the plane touched down, my attention switched to the doors. As they opened,

I held my breath until I saw Mum appear and walk down the steps. She looked up at the viewing gallery and waved. I ran into the terminal building where I looked through the iron railings into the baggage hall below. As soon as I saw Mum pick up her bag, I set off again, sprinting down the stairs, timing my arrival so that I threw myself into her arms the moment she came through the arrival gate.

The scene sticks with me because airports were always happy places for me. Dad and I would make countless trips from our home in Damansara Heights to Subang to meet Mum, and they all ended with this warm feeling of being reunited with her.

A few years later, Dad and I started making trips to the Weld department store in Kuala Lumpur. It had a huge record department with wooden racks holding albums stacked vertically so that we could flip through the records from front to back. We would go there on a Sunday morning between church (which I hated) and lunch, which we normally had at one of those old colonial restaurants like the Station Hotel or the Coliseum.

On one occasion I was standing on tiptoe on a stool flicking through the albums when I laid eyes on a special record.

'Dad, Dad!' I jumped down from the stool (we were there so regularly that the staff called it 'Anthony's Stool') and ran across to him as he looked through the Dean Martin section. In my hand I had an album that I held up to him.

'Can we buy it?' I asked hopefully.

He nodded. I was hopping with excitement. It was my first record: the Supremes' *Supremes A' Go-Go*. We'd heard 'You Can't Hurry Love' on Patrick Teoh's radio show the previous weekend and I'd been itching to get the album ever since. In the holidays, if I dusted and organized Dad's records, I was allowed to play them on our Grundig stereo system. He adored the classics – Dean Martin, Sinatra, Bing Crosby, Sammy Davis Jr – all the singers from that golden era.

The music I associate with Mum is Chopin's Nocturnes. I loved to listen to her playing these beautiful pieces on the upright Yamaha piano in the living room. As well as Chopin, she'd play Mozart and Beethoven, and whenever and wherever we moved to, the piano would always have its own corner. Mum arranged for piano and violin teachers to come to the house and teach me but if I was going to learn to play something, I was going to do it on my own or with my mum. Her musical talents and methods definitely rubbed off on me because, like her, I can pick things up by ear and I always preferred to learn like that.

When she put on a record, Mum would choose an artist like Dionne Warwick or Carole King. She had more progressive tastes than my dad but the most influential thing was how much they both loved music. That has always stayed with me.

Another thing that has stayed with me is Dad's love of sport. He would watch every single sport shown on television in Malaysia. He followed teams and events with intensity and was a tireless supporter of underdogs – whenever there was an uneven contest, he always sided with the least-fancied team or player.

He would take me to sporting events all over the country and together we watched many matches on the television. I followed Brazil from a young age. Their teams of the early seventies were unbelievable: Pelé, Rivelino, Jairzinho, Carlos Alberto. All of them were outstanding players and the 1970 World Cup side were arguably the best team in history. Dad and I would also watch *Star Soccer*, which showed English football games with a six-month delay. For some reason the games always seemed to feature teams from the Midlands (like West Brom, Wolverhampton, Birmingham and Aston Villa). It was horrific football – lumping the ball up to the centre forward, a scrappy midfield with no skill or tactics, muddy pitches and bone-crunching tackles. It was all about getting rid of the ball as quickly as possible without a hint of a bigger game plan. There was none of the elegance or style you got with the other teams I'd watched, like Brazil. The contrast in the way they played football couldn't have been more marked.

Then, one day in 1974, I saw another *Star Soccer* game and my opinion of English football changed for ever. The match was Aston Villa against West Ham. I hadn't seen the London team before and it was as if I *was* watching Brazil, only in the mud and greyness of Birmingham. West Ham played from the back and they had a plan and a style – passing the ball around to create openings. Trevor Brooking, Alan Devonshire, Frank Lampard, Pat Holland and, my favourite, Clyde Best. They had the skill and fluidity of the Brazilian superstars. I decided there and then that I'd support them.

Although I loved sport, I wasn't really any good at it initially. At the age of eight, I bought my first football boots and decided that being a goalkeeper was the easiest position to establish myself in. As long as I was playing, I was happy. Then at about ten something changed – suddenly I could play.

For my birthday around that time, my uncle bought me a Philips shortwave radio. There were no live games on the television so every Saturday night I'd tune in to the BBC World Service and Paddy Feeny's *Sportsworld*. The programme covered the afternoon's English First Division matches. Of course, in those days they all kicked off at 3.00 on Saturday afternoon – there were no matches on Sundays. The radio had a couple of shortwave bands, medium wave and FM, and I had to hold it up at all sorts of weird angles to get a reception (the best place was next to the fridge). I thought, 'Wow, what a piece of kit.'

Every weekend during the season, that's what I'd do – Saturday nights were all about the football from 11.00 p.m. till 2.00 a.m. West Ham rarely featured as the live game but regular updates meant I could follow them. Plus I got *Shoot!* magazine for all the latest news. At the start of each season they included a wall chart showing each of the leagues and cut-out labels for each of the teams. Armed with these, I changed the league positions after the results came in every Saturday night. I had a favourite team in each league as well. Believe it or not, QPR were my 'second' team at the time. Gerry Francis, Stan Bowles, Mick Thomas and Rodney Marsh made the club almost as attractive as West Ham.

I was sports mad, like my dad, and we went to just about every sporting event we could in Malaysia. There's a football competition called the Merdeka Tournament (Pestabola Merdeka) which used to happen every year. All the South East Asia teams played a series of games over the course of a week. One year – it may have been 1974 or 1975 – we didn't miss a single game.

We'd also go to the motor racing every year, at a track at

Batu Tiga, and watch Formula Two and MotoGP. It was three days of very noisy track racing that I lapped up. There were some legendary South East Asian and Japanese drivers: Albert Poon (later 'Sir') and Harvey Yap were my local heroes. I thought of those days as I walked to the track at the first Malaysian Grand Prix many years later, surrounded by the revving of Formula One engines. Just like the tuck box, the memory brought tears to my eyes as I thought about my dad and how he'd have loved to have been there to witness such a momentous event.

When the Hockey World Cup came to Malaysia in 1975 it was the first time a world championship of any kind had been held there; the whole country went mad for it. We went to every game. Dad supported India so I did too, though it got a bit awkward when India met Malaysia in the semi-final and beat them (after extra time), going on to win the World Cup. Of course, in those days, the pitches were grass, so when it rained and the games were called off they were rearranged for a morning during the week instead of the evening. On those occasions, Dad would be driving me to school and I'd pester him, 'Let's go, let's go, let's go. We don't want to miss a match.'

Finally he'd say 'OK' and we'd go. He criticized me for being useless at school but he'd also take me to a hockey match on a school day!

Alongside his great love of sport and music, Dad was quite studious, reserved, disciplined and highly principled. He was a doctor working for the World Health Organization, in charge of the programme to eradicate malaria and dengue fever. He had started out as an engineer before switching to become an architect and then finally settling on medicine. His family were from Goa and were upper middle class, but he grew up in Calcutta and went to boarding school when he was five. He did well – excelled at sport – and graduated with distinction. After his medical training, he was sent to Malaysia and met my mum on a blind date. He never left.

I loved my dad and his dedication to the WHO programme, and his political ideas have had a huge influence on me. He was devoted to the idea of public health for the public good and wouldn't go anywhere near private medicine. He was naturally curious, always wanting to know how things worked and wanting to understand the world – he bought every encyclopaedia known to man and made sure I read them. I didn't love him for that at the time, but I think that's where my curiosity stems from. I still have the first encyclopaedia he bought me: *The Book of Knowledge* published by Marshall Cavendish.

Funnily enough, I was at a convocation ceremony at MAHSA University in Kuala Lumpur in March 2017 and met a nurse called Ajimah Hassan, who had worked with my dad in the early seventies. She told me that he was small but athletically built (which I was too for a while, believe it or not). She also told me that he was a heavy smoker who loved his coffee – he would often come to chat to the nurses after work over a cup of Nescafé.

'He was so approachable,' she said, 'all us nurses felt that we could talk to him about anything at all. It was more like having a sympathetic big brother than a boss.'

At that moment, I felt so proud of him, and so proud to be his son.

While my father was reserved, Ena, my mum, was out-going and infectiously energetic. She loved talking and getting friends together for a party. The house always seemed to be full of music and people: the Ink Spots, Winifred Atwell and the Platters. One day she found out that the legendary singer-songwriter Ray Charles was in Malaysia. Those were the days when no one had any security so she rang him at his hotel, introduced herself and said, 'We're having a party. Do you want to come over?' And he did. He made straight for the piano and played 'Georgia on My Mind' – the song still makes my spine tingle. Many years later, when I was president of Warner Music in Asia, I met Ray Charles when he came back to Malaysia and he remembered everything: my mum, the piano and the party.

Mum's surname was also Fernandez – but with a 'z' rather than an 's'. She was born in Malacca and I think I inherited some of my entrepreneurial spirit from her side of the family. They were a lot less well-off than Dad's: her father was a car salesman who, during the Japanese occupation in the Second World War, was regularly put in jail for communicating with the British. He was a risk-taker – just like Mum.

After she finished school, Mum became a music teacher at a convent school but then her sister introduced her to Tupperware and her entrepreneurial gene was triggered. The business model was simple: you invited friends and family over to show them Tupperware products and got commission on any sales made. It was popular and Mum loved it – why wouldn't she? It allowed her to throw parties and be an entrepreneur at the same time. She was so good at it that she rose through the ranks from selling agent to running Tupperware in Malaysia. With the job she was always off on field trips to see reps or pitch new products and one day this brought about my first experience on an aeroplane, a trip to Penang on Tupperware business. We'd always gone on the ferry before – driven to Butterworth and then taken the boat across to Penang Island – but this time we flew from Kuala Lumpur to Penang. For a nine-year-old boy it was an unbelievable thrill.

After that we'd often go on trips to visit dealers around Malaysia, and we'd make up songs to motivate them. 'Gotta Tupper Feeling Up in My Head' was the name of one. I still write songs today – not about Tupperware – and that's because of her.

Mum was the dominant personality in the house. She was at the heart of everything we did and drove us forward. She was determined I was going to be a doctor – the family story goes that as soon as I was out of the womb she hung a stethoscope round my neck. Even my first toy was a doctor's kit. But later it was to become the source of a lot of friction between us.

Even as a kid I could see that Mum adored me. Dad was less demonstrative. When I was eleven, I was made captain of our school football team, and in one match I scored five goals against a Japanese team. Dad was watching, and when I came up to him at the end of the game I thought, 'He has to praise me this time.' But all he said was: 'You're a real hog – you didn't pass the ball once.' I was devastated. At the same time, he rarely missed a game. He was devoted, but he found it hard to verbalize his feelings and give any praise.

13

Mum, on the other hand, thought I was perfect, always seeking to show me off to her friends. Every time she had a party, I'd be called into the living room and told to play the piano. I had a medley of songs which I rattled off while Mum beamed with pride.

Her exuberance and generosity extended to her attitude to money. She was extravagant to the point of recklessness, which meant that quite often I was spoilt. My Aunty Girly (we still call her that and it drives her mad as her real name is Enid) tells me that Christmas was always awkward. We'd gather as a family at Mum and Dad's and there were presents for all the kids around the tree. My cousins, she says, got 'ordinary presents' like a teddy bear or a book, but I usually got something bigger and the other children would want mine. One time, she reminds me, Mum came back from the UK and gave me a pure crystal football. It wasn't like I could take it outside and play with it but, for whatever reason, she wanted me to have it. Aunty Girly would tell Mum that she was spoiling me, but Mum would say: 'I can't help it. I just can't say "no" to him!'

My dad was more frugal and less showy. I like to think I absorbed the best of both approaches from my parents but I am probably more influenced by Mum's attitude when it comes to personal spending and by Dad when it comes to running a business. I love to spend money on entertaining people but I'm also an accountant at heart so I understand how to control money. I think it's fair to say I run my businesses better than I run my own finances!

For all the joy it created, Mum's love of luxury sometimes got us into difficulties and once we had to move out of a house I loved because we were in over our heads financially. The first house I remember was a terrace house and it was split in two like a London maisonette. We lived on the top floor and on the bottom floor there was an industrious Jewish couple who went on to own the Tower Records franchise in Malaysia and the Coffee Bean and Tea Leaf chain. Then we moved to Ampang to a huge colonial-style house which Dad got through his job with the WHO. It had a garden with enough space to mark out a football pitch; I thought houses couldn't get any better. But, after a period, we bought our own house in a new area called Damansara Heights. This is the house that is most vivid to me. It was the scene of the wildest parties, of the most memorable Christmases and where my greatest childhood memories were formed. My sister arrived about this time too, so even if I was a bit jealous of the attention she got, the atmosphere was happy.

We moved a couple more times in Kuala Lumpur and ended up in a neighbourhood where there were five or six kids, some older and some younger than me, who I used to hang out with every evening. We'd meet on some land nearby that hadn't been developed and play badminton, football and any other ball game that you can imagine. Mum would go mad complaining that I wasn't working hard enough and was worried I would never become a doctor. But I wasn't exactly studious – I was smart enough, but I only did the minimum academically needed to get by. Like a lot of boys at that age, I couldn't see the point of memorizing things for the sake of it.

As I headed towards the age of eleven, I started to understand that there were problems in my mum's life.

Her mood would swing from periods of high intensity to chronic inactivity. Sometimes she was really on it – she'd discover from somewhere or other that 5.00 a.m. was the best time to study, so she'd wake me up at 5.00 a.m. and make me study history with her. Then other times she'd be stuck in her room for what seemed like months on end.

When she was in the low phase, Dad would send her to hospital for treatment. Through my eleven-year-old eyes it didn't make any sense: home was where she should be. I used to fight with him, not understanding why she had to go, why she had to leave us. As the months went by, the low phases seemed to get longer and I felt her absence more, craving the time she'd re-emerge from her room or return from the hospital.

When Mum was down, the house was down too: it felt cold, empty and far too still. The piano was silent and Dad moved quietly around; my piano medley got rusty as friends and parties became distant memories. All I wanted was to hear my mum humming a tune or for her to chase me around the house, trying to catch me.

Dad was strict with me and when Mum was away I didn't enjoy the same freedoms. He sat me down to read and do my homework without the lightness that Mum brought to the job.

One day, Dad and I had a furious argument in the dining room. Mum had just been taken off to hospital again and I was so angry that I couldn't control myself. We faced off on opposite sides of the dining-room table. All the frustration, sadness and the fear of another long spell of life without Mum came to the surface.

'Dad, don't send her away! She should be here. I hate it when she's gone,' I shouted.

'Anthony, it's for her own good; she'll be better in the long run,' Dad said, trying to calm me down.

'I don't care about the long run.'

'Listen, she has to go to hospital to get better.'

'You're just cruel and I hate you,' I snapped back.

Dad clearly wasn't impressed. 'Don't ever say that. You, son, need to show some respect. Go to your room,' he bellowed.

'No,' I replied stubbornly.

He never raised his hand to me but I thought he might then. He was furious. I stood in front of him, defying him properly for the first time.

Dad looked like he didn't know what to do for a second; then, he did what he always did when he needed an answer, he turned round to the bookcase and picked out a book. He flicked through until he found what he was looking for and slapped the open book down on the dining table.

'Read that. And then go to your room.' He walked out.

I don't think I'd ever seen him so angry. Looking back, I realize he was worried and perhaps scared. Though so different, he and Mum loved each other deeply.

After he'd gone, I walked up to the table and looked at the open page. There was an entry for Manic Depression. Reading the article, seeing her diagnosed in black and white with little idea about treatment, made me understand just how serious her condition was. I found Dad not long after and told him he was right.

My reaction to this sad news about Mum was to throw

myself into sport even harder. Dad encouraged me. Beneath his aloof exterior he was a passionate man.

Perhaps because Mum was suffering so badly or maybe because she was still determined that I should become a doctor, my parents arranged a family trip to England in August 1976 to visit Epsom College, a school with a rich medical academic history. We flew to London and stayed in the White House Hotel near Great Portland Street, and from there we made the trip to Epsom in Surrey. I was completely uninterested in seeing the school and didn't understand why they were considering sending me there.

I was made to sit a test and I must have passed because we were taken on a tour of the school and grounds. The only question I asked was whether they played football; I was told they played only rugby and hockey, so I felt sorry for the boys who went there. No football!

The next day Mum took me to Selfridges and bought me a West Ham top. I was so proud to wear that shiny claret and blue shirt that the previous day's disappointment faded away. Dad tried to get tickets for a West Ham game while we were in England but unfortunately it didn't work out. I did have one more unforgettable moment on the trip, though. Mum was now working for Pyrex and had a meeting in Sunderland. We travelled up on the train and, while she went to her meeting, Dad took me to Roker Park. It was so much bigger than any sports ground I'd seen in Malaysia. Even without a crowd, the stadium made me dizzy and I got my first feeling of what the atmosphere at an English First Division game must be like. Up to that point, I'd just imagined the grounds from listening to the radio and seeing highlights on television; to experience a stadium up close made me realize just how intense, loud and exciting watching a real game would be.

When we got back home, I soon forgot about the trip to Epsom. A whole year passed and I spent every evening playing football in my West Ham top as late as I could before Mum would call me in for dinner or the sun would set.

Then, one day in July 1977, Mum and Dad appeared at my bedroom door. This was unusual but as I was bouncing up and down on my bed, I assumed they were coming up to tell me off. Instead, Dad told me that in September I would be going to the English school. The school that didn't play football.

2. Outward Bound

Soundtrack: 'Lonely Boy' by Andrew Gold

My parents drove me to the airport in early September 1977. I wasn't scared – in fact I was thrilled to be flying by myself for the first time at the age of thirteen.

As soon as we arrived I was handed over to a stewardess who took me off to a waiting room to sit in before my Qantas flight was called. The farewell with Mum and Dad and my little sister was offset by my excitement at flying solo. The thrill of take-off, brought on by the roar of the engines as they reach full power and the juddering of the 747 as it hurtles down the runway, is a feeling I still love today. I remember the steep lift-off vividly, my ears popping as we smashed through the clouds and into the clear blue sky. I was sustained by pure adrenaline for most of the flight; I don't remember sleeping a wink. We stopped off in Bahrain but I stayed on the plane, not wanting to leave it until I absolutely had to.

When I finally got off the plane at Heathrow, I looked around and my first thought was: 'God, everyone's white here!' Whereas flying had been fun, arriving by myself was scary. As I followed the signs to the baggage reclaim area, the crush and size of the crowd made me feel tiny – everything at the airport was on such a grand scale. I'd been there before but visiting somewhere with your parents is a different experience to arriving by yourself. I felt nervous and vulnerable. And I now faced a lonely journey to Epsom on a coach which the school had told my parents was a Green Line bus number 727. I didn't know where I had to go to get on it and had no idea how long the journey was. The only remaining instruction was to get off at the Spread Eagle pub on Epsom High Street.

I waited by the luggage carousel, eyes fixed on the bags appearing out of the hole in the wall, nervously watching as other passengers picked up their suitcases and walked away.

I managed to find the 727 bus departing from outside Terminal 2. The driver put my suitcase in the luggage hold, waited for more passengers and then we were off. As we drove along the A roads through Teddington, Kingston and then out into the Surrey countryside, I couldn't believe how green everything was. It was also crowded in a way that I hadn't experienced before – roads busy with people, cars, motorbikes and lorries. The bus seemed to be constantly stopping and starting while I sat anxiously looking out for the next stop.

The driver kindly let me know when we got to the Spread Eagle on Epsom High Street and unloaded my suitcase. As the bus pulled away to continue its journey to Gatwick, I looked around, not sure what to do next. A teenage girl was walking by so I asked her directions to the college. She held up her hand to me which I thought might be an English way of saying hello, until she said, 'Go home. We don't want your sort here.'

Welcome to England.

Eventually, an elderly man pointed me in the right direction and I started on the final leg of my journey. The suitcase was heavy and, of course, back then they had no wheels, so I carried it slowly along the narrow pavements through Epsom and beyond into the leafier outer reaches of the town until I finally saw the sign that pointed to my home for the next six years.

After the flight, the bus trip and the two-mile walk, I was knackered, hungry and cold. I dragged my suitcase on to the campus of Epsom College where I saw the main building for the first time on my own. It was daunting. Sitting on top of a slight incline, it stretched about 500 feet either side of a main entrance that had huge double wooden doors. The doors were topped with a crenelated tower and a flagpole proudly displaying the Union Jack. Outlining the entrance was a white stone arch that contrasted with the deep-red brick and the dark leaded windows on the rest of the building. To a thirteen-year-old boy from Kuala Lumpur the set-up did not feel welcoming. If I'd felt tiny at Heathrow, I felt microscopic now.

I opened the huge doors and found a master who pointed me in the direction of my allotted house, Holman House, whose colours were red and white. He told me to hurry up and get changed because dinner was in ten minutes. I raced back across the campus and down the hill I'd just walked up, to Holman House. I climbed up the stairs and found my dormitory: twenty beds split ten and ten running along the walls of a long room. I grabbed a spare bed, opened my suitcase and pulled out my uniform. The other boys in the room looked at me with curiosity and then began to laugh as I struggled to knot my tie – something I never got much better at. Eventually, a fellow pupil, Roddy Williams, took pity on me and helped. Worried that I wouldn't be able to tie it again by myself, I kept the same knot tied for my first week, just loosening it enough to pull it over my head at night and then tightening it in the morning when I put it back on. My new friend, Roddy, and I started talking about football and I began to feel better.

Late and hungry, we ran downstairs to go to the main building for dinner. We were so engrossed in our conversation and worried about being late that we took the shortest way possible across the grounds. Out of nowhere, we heard a man screaming at us at the top of his voice.

'You! You two horrible boys! Get off the grass this instant or you'll be in detention before you know it.'

We froze, terrified. Mr Parker, a history master who looked frightening in his suit and black scholar's gown, glided up and gave us a telling-off, to the enjoyment of all the other boys hurrying to dinner. Roddy and I bowed our heads and shuffled off to the dining room. To top off an exhausting and upsetting day at my new school, I had been publicly embarrassed by one of the first masters I'd met.

My parents never told me explicitly why they sent me to Epsom but it wasn't long before their motive became clear. The school opened in 1855 to house widows of the medical profession and to provide education for their sons. The Royal Medical Foundation, set up by Dr John Propert, was the body that raised the money and built the campus; and when the school opened it was called the Royal Medical Benevolent College. Initially, there were a hundred boys but the number of children grew slowly. When I arrived there would have been nearly 600 boys. I've been told that Epsom College has educated more doctors than any other school in England – and, some say, the world. But despite my mum's hopes, I wasn't destined to become another doctor and add to Epsom's impressive medical history.

I spent the first week trying to work out how to navigate around the campus, learning about the history of the building and trying to get used to things which seemed bizarre. It felt so strange eating in a dining hall with over five hundred other boys and sleeping in a dorm with nineteen others. There were two matrons who looked after our washing: we just threw dirty clothes into a huge wicker basket at one end of the dorm and, a few days later, they'd reappear washed and ironed. Nothing in my new life was familiar and there wasn't much of the comfort of home about it. When we showered in the morning, the water was often lukewarm or freezing cold because there was only a limited amount of hot water and the sixth-formers always went first. Homesickness, already hovering, landed hard on me. I missed home. Life here was so different and I felt so far away from anything I recognized.

The strangeness continued in my first games class. We played rugby which seemed all wrong to me: picking up an egg-shaped ball and running into the opposition players who tried to bring you down to the ground. It was the polar opposite of the game I loved. In my first game, a boy on the other team got the ball and started to run down the wing. I was fast then and easily caught up with him. Everyone was screaming at me to tackle him but, as far as I was concerned, I couldn't tackle him like I would in football because that would just count as tripping him up. So I tracked him until he put the ball down and scored a try. I really didn't get it at all.

After games we all piled into the changing rooms and were told to shower together. That freaked me out completely. Sharing a corridor of showers with thirty other boys seemed very weird.

Once we'd got back into our uniforms I looked around for somewhere to put my dirty kit. An older boy pointed at the wire cages we'd hung our uniforms in while we played rugby. I was amazed. Unlike our uniform, the kit stayed in the cage for at least three or four sessions before it was washed, so if we came in from a really wet or muddy game, it would just sit there mouldering until we came to wear it again. Pulling it on was revolting.

The first school away match came that first Saturday. We all climbed on coaches and started the long drive to Merchant Taylors' School near Watford. One of the boys was carrying an Adidas bag on which he'd written *Jairzinho*.

'You know Jairzinho?' I asked the boy, whose name was Déj Mahoney. He was the one I'd tracked down the touchline rather than tackled. He looked at me like I'd lived in the woods all my life and we immediately started talking about the great Brazilian players, which led on to swapping stories about our favourite football teams and stars. Oddly enough, football had helped me to establish myself in a rugby school and I made a lifelong friend in Déj. So many of my friendships date back to Epsom, and Déj and I are still in touch, as I am with lots of school friends, even from the Alice Smith School I went to in Kuala Lumpur.

Despite not having a clue how to play rugby, I threw myself into it. It was sport after all and I was quick and had good hands. One afternoon I was playing for my house team and I scored four tries because I was difficult to get hold of. A teacher must have noticed me because I was put in the A team squad, although I only made the B team. It was the second year before I made the A team.

Despite calls home, I still missed Mum and Dad, my friends and relations. Just before the half-term break of that very long first term, I rang my mum. It would turn out to be a prophetic conversation.

I said, 'Mum, I want to come home.'

'It's too expensive.'

'But it's horrible here and I miss everyone.'

'It's too expensive, Anthony, you'll have to stay until Christmas and come home then.'

'But why is it so expensive? Why can't they make it cheap?'

'Flying's expensive and we can't afford to bring you home every seven weeks.'

I was angry.

'Well, I'm going to make it cheap.'

It didn't seem that big a deal at the time. I was furious that I couldn't make it home to see my parents and friends, and could not understand that money should play such a big part in preventing my happiness.

Looking back, of course, this is when my idea – my life-long mission – that everyone should be able to fly was first hatched. I instinctively understood that the cost of the plane ticket was the barrier to being with my family. I understood that not being able to afford to fly was a cause of a lot of unhappiness. I don't think AirAsia would have been born if this seed hadn't been planted decades earlier in Epsom.

The homesickness passed quickly after those first few

testing weeks and within a couple of terms my life at Epsom was busy. I had a solid group of friends who shared my love of pranks; we played tricks on the teachers but also on each other, always mucking about in lessons and never taking them too seriously. There were the traditional challenges to take on, like climbing over Holman House, which involved escaping from a first-floor window, shimmying up a drainpipe, using as many window ledges and footholds as you could find, and then clambering on to the roof before reversing the journey on the other side of the house. When I look at the height and the difficulty of the climb now it makes me feel a bit sick. I'm sure the boys aren't allowed to do it any more but back in the seventies no one really minded and, as it turned out, no one got hurt.

Best of all, there was sport to immerse myself in every day. Hockey was a big deal at the school and at least I understood *that*, having watched all those games with my dad and having played a bit with the boys back in Malaysia. In fact, Déj told me recently that when I started at Epsom he could tell I was a natural at hockey. I had good hand–eye coordination and although I was small I was also muscular so could hold my own when players tried to tackle me. As with football, I was quick and I had an instinct for goal. After one of the World Cup matches in Malaysia, Dad and I had approached the Indian team and I'd been given an autographed hockey stick (a Vampire) by the Indian captain. It was my pride and joy and I played with it at Epsom – making sure everyone saw the signatures.

Although I knew how to play hockey, we played it in the

spring term at Epsom after rugby in the autumn had finished. And that confused me. I was used to playing hockey in the Malaysian heat, not the freezing cold with hands so stiff they were unable to grip the stick properly. The pitches were either waterlogged (meaning the ball constantly got stuck in the mud) or were frozen (meaning we all slid around). In my first winter term, it snowed. I was baffled – I'd never seen snow before. I asked a classmate how long snow usually lasted, and then I was even more confused when the white blanket disappeared overnight. Once, when the pitches were covered in snow, we were sent to the Epsom Public Swimming Baths. I was naturally expecting to swim but when we got there we found a maple-wood floor had been placed over the pool and we played indoor hockey on it. If anything, this was stranger to me than playing in the freezing cold.

In the summer term, cricket and athletics dominated our sports lessons. In my first couple of years I focused on athletics because I was a top sprinter – becoming Epsom School's Champion at fourteen. Although I was short, I was lightning fast. Unfortunately, I never really grew; as the other boys' legs got longer, mine stayed the same and I couldn't match them. That wasn't a problem on the rugby field because I was still quick and my size made me difficult to pull down, but over a straight hundred metres I didn't have the stride length to match some of the bigger boys.

I got into cricket after that. It was one of those sports where I was either brilliant – scoring a century – or terrible – getting out first ball. There was rarely anything in between, which frustrated the Epsom sports masters. I had a strange batting action which meant that the back-swing of the bat went out to the right and then forward rather than straight back and forward. Roy Moody, my house master and cricket coach, spent hours trying to correct the problem but I never learned. All it meant was that I found it difficult to 'play straight' – it didn't stop me scoring a lot when I was on form but I often got bowled out needlessly. As it happened I had the same swing with a hockey stick but perhaps because I was usually in full flight when I went for a shot on goal, that mattered less.

Once I'd settled into the school, I found I was popular but I always felt there was a certain distance between me and the other kids. For the life of me I couldn't work out why. One day, a good friend of mine, Charlie Hunt, a day student, invited boarders back to his home for a party. I was annoyed that I hadn't been invited and assumed I wasn't included because I was a different skin colour. When I asked him about it years later, it turns out that he hadn't invited me because he thought I didn't know how to use a knife and fork! He didn't want to embarrass me because he thought I had grown up in a treehouse or something. At the time no one had heard of Malaysia – I used to say that it was between Singapore and Thailand and, even then, people couldn't really place it. I do wonder whether, deep down, the shock of finding out that people knew next to nothing about Malaysia is one of my motivations for working so hard to put it and the whole Association of South East Asian Nations (ASEAN) region on the map. AirAsia is certainly helping with that but it's a slow process.

I did witness some clear instances of racism: the school

was overwhelmingly white and the culture at the time was just different. Television programmes like *Till Death Us Do Part* and *Love Thy Neighbour* portrayed almost aggressively racist views, so it's not much of a surprise that I was called names like 'wog', particularly on the rugby pitch. I don't remember being offended or hurt, it just made me play better and harder. It's as if the insults spurred me on to prove everybody wrong and I got more satisfaction from that than any other kind of reaction.

The academic atmosphere was quite intense at Epsom but the routine at school was good for me: having a predictable timetable brought stability and meant that I looked forward to certain parts of the day and the week. Breakfast was my favourite meal – there was an endless supply of horrific sausages that I'd wrap up in bread and wash down with a few bowls of cereal. After breakfast, we'd have a morning of lessons, which was the bit I didn't particularly enjoy, but every day after lunch there would be sport – except on Wednesdays when we joined a branch of the service cadets of our choice. I chose the navy because the army guys were way too serious; the navy was where all the pranks and fun were to be had.

One Wednesday my friends and I broke into the navy store cupboard and I nicked one of each of the achievement badges and sewed them on to my cadet jersey sleeve. That afternoon, we had the big AGI (Annual General Inspection) parade in front of a rear admiral or some other high-ranking navy guy who was of course amazed by my accomplishments. He asked me all sorts of questions about how I'd got this or that award but I didn't have a clue and had to bluff my way through. He gave up asking quite quickly.

As well as Wednesday afternoons, I enjoyed the weekends. After lessons on Saturday mornings, there were always matches against other schools in the area and, as I got older, I played rugby, hockey and cricket for Epsom.

On Sundays, full boarders were supposed to go to the chapel but I said I was Roman Catholic and that my dad didn't want me to go to a Church of England service. The school would have allowed me to attend mass elsewhere but, naturally, I didn't go; I just enjoyed some free time on Sunday morning.

I spent the weekends reading a pile of biographies and autobiographies; perhaps because, like Mum, I am interested in people. Some of the books I read at Epsom shaped my outlook on life. The ones that really stand out and had the greatest influence over me were biographies of Alexander the Great, Thomas Edison and Robert the Bruce, and Antonia Fraser's *Cromwell, Our Chief of Men*.

Alexander the Great became a hero of mine because he was so ambitious. He tried to create a world free of racial barriers and separate cultures by forcing ethnic groups to inter-marry. He believed in democracy and, above all else, he was a mummy's boy! I was captivated by Thomas Edison's life, inspired by the sheer number of ideas and innovations he produced. Studying his approach and life's work illustrated to me the value of innovation, something that has influenced the way I run my businesses ever since. I constantly ask myself: 'What do we need that we don't have?' 'What could we do to make this easier for the passenger or customer?' 'What could the staff work on to change the way our business works?' Like Edison, I never want to accept the status quo but try to find a new and better way of doing something. The main lesson I took from Robert the Bruce was the importance of tenacity and perseverance: he never gave up and I have the same determination in my work and life. Journalists often say that they tire of writing about my persistence as I pursue what I want at all costs. Finally, Oliver Cromwell's republican views have had a meaningful influence on me; I believe that everyone should have a chance at life and if the system of government in charge gives one group of people advantage over another, that doesn't seem fair to me.

Reading about and understanding these lives had a powerful effect as I passed through my teenage years. Some of the core business principles I run my companies by can be traced in part back to these books. I believe in a multicultural workforce based on meritocracy; I value persistence and admire it in people around me; and I am always looking to innovate in my companies, encouraging colleagues to come up with a new way of tackling a problem.

Through these men and their biographies, I really got the history bug; it's still my favourite subject (even though the history teacher had been the one to shout at me on my first day). When I make speeches, I always look to the past to find my themes and examples. The lessons learned in those pages have stuck with me.

I still liked music but I only got to listen to it via the cassettes I borrowed from friends or had sent from home. I tracked down every musical reference I could out of sheer curiosity. When ABBA released 'Fernando' my friends thought it was hilarious to change the line to 'Do you hear the drums, Fernandes?' I sort of enjoyed the joke but got

Dad to send me the album *Arrival* on cassette. Only to find it thirty years later, still in my tuck box.

My interest in music gave me a creative advantage and strength that some people lack – I was always on the look-out for new sounds, a trait which came to help me later during my time at Warner. Although never very happy in the classroom, I wasn't a slouch academically; it was just that I was much more comfortable in the music room or on the sports fields where I was free to express myself. I played the piano as much as I could, though I still hated having lessons because I think I understood, even at that age, that I learned best by doing it myself. I pick things up quickly but I like to be able to see the immediate effect of what I'm being shown or taught; learning is an active and interactive process, and I learn particularly fast if I'm able to get my hands dirty. Most other subjects at school bored me because I couldn't see the point of passive learning, which dominated the teaching style. I wasn't interested in other subjects beside history and music; certainly not the sciences that were supposedly going to get me into medical school.

As I grew up at Epsom my main interests revolved around either sport, planes or cars (and sometimes the girls who'd just been admitted into the sixth form). There was a young biology teacher called Mike Hobbs who owned a Mini. One night we carried his car and put it on the centre line of the First XV rugby pitch. I can't remember why we did it – perhaps because he'd wound us up particularly badly or just because we were in search of a good prank. We had a lesson with him the next day and we couldn't stop laughing the whole way through it. Finally, he cracked and asked us what was so funny. We led him out to the rugby pitches to show him the car. Our laughter quickly turned to bewilderment and then panic as we saw that the car had disappeared. We had to explain what we'd done but had no explanation as to why the car wasn't there. Class detention followed. The next day we saw Hobbs drive on to the campus in his Mini, smiling and whistling as he parked and got out of it. He told me much later that he'd heard us whispering suspiciously in the night and followed to see what we were up to. After we'd gone back to bed, he'd driven the car off campus and parked it in a neighbouring street so it would look like the car had vanished or been stolen. We had to admit he had out-pranked us.

Apart from staging pranks, I'd use my spare time to make trips to Heathrow as often as possible. Charlie Hunt and I would catch the 727 Green Line bus I took on my first day of school and we'd go plane spotting, watching the planes land from the viewing platform on the Queen's Building. My interest in planes was growing and I loved being able to share my passion with someone like Charlie, who got it.

I sailed through school until my O-level year. In early January, with the new term just started, Dad called me. This wasn't unusual: we'd been talking a lot more frequently since Mum had started going through another bad patch but his voice sounded different this time, quieter perhaps.

He said, 'Mum's really sick. It's really, really bad. She might not survive this time.'

Even then, I didn't take it too seriously because there

had been other times like this when she'd been really ill. And Mum was a force of nature. Her energy was infectious when she was feeling well and those were the times I focused on. Her knack for entrepreneurship and business had created a huge success of the Tupperware job, so much so that she financed my education at an expensive English public school and provided a comfortable lifestyle for her family. But now there were real problems with her kidneys, which in turn seemed to be affecting her heart.

I called every day to check and the reports I got back were that she was getting better. Then, one day, I was sitting in a geography class – bored as usual – when the school secretary walked into the classroom and asked for me to follow her.

It was unusual to be pulled out of lessons so as I walked behind her to the school office I was dreading every step that took me closer to the phone. I picked up the receiver and was greeted by my dad, crying.

'She's gone,' he said.

And with those words, my whole world collapsed. She was only forty-eight years old and I was only fifteen – at that age you think your parents are indestructible.

My dad, who had never really outwardly shown much emotion before, was still crying over the phone and, being so far apart, there was nothing we could do to help each other. I asked whether I should come home. He quietly said: 'No, focus on your O levels.'

I'd spoken to Mum a few days before she passed away. She was concerned about my grades and the mock exams coming up but we hadn't discussed her illness. In fact, the last time I'd actually seen her back in Kuala Lumpur, we had parted badly. We'd had a row because I'd told my parents that I wasn't going to do physics, chemistry and biology for A level but had decided on biology, economics and history instead. The fallout turned into World War Three – my mum was angrier than I'd ever seen her before. When I left KL she was still pissed off with me and she just put me in a car and said 'bye' without a hug or any other sign of affection. In the end, they forced me to do the sciences but I told them that if they made me do them, I'd fail.

So the last time I'd seen Mum before she passed away wasn't a happy memory and I didn't get to say goodbye on the phone when we spoke either. It makes me sad to this day that the last time I actually saw her we parted on such bad terms.

I couldn't stay at school while Mum was being buried thousands of miles away so I packed a suitcase and went to stay with my Uncle John, Mum's sister's husband, in Braintree, Essex, for a week. I needed to be alone, out of sight of my school friends, and John was really good to me. He was strict – an old-fashioned English type who wouldn't take any argument – but we grew close during that week. He had a huge room full of radio communications equipment, including radios you could use to listen in to the pilots' frequencies as they talked to air traffic control. He was a bit of a plane-spotter too and I think we made a few trips to the airport that week. Staying in Essex with John was about the best thing I could have done to distract me from my grief. After a week, my uncle told me that I had better return and I reluctantly took the train to Epsom. Everyone at the school was good to me when I got back and my friends rallied round, trying to cheer me up.

After a difficult term, I travelled back home to Malaysia for the summer. The silence in the house was unbearable – without Mum there, we had no visitors, the piano was silent and there were no crazy schemes and plans. For the first few days I felt like I was waiting for her to come back to kick-start the life and noise in the house but then I realized that she wasn't coming. So I decided to step into her shoes and did everything I could to make up for her not being there: inviting friends round, playing the piano, putting on records and trying to get the energy up. My sister was only two when I left for Epsom and was still young when I came back for the summer but that was the time when we started to bond properly.

As soon as I got back to school after the summer break, I transformed as a sports player from a pretty good all-rounder to something of a superstar. Up until O-level year I had been doing well across the board – in the A team for hockey and rugby and pretty good at cricket too. Then after Mum died I started channelling all of my grieving energy into my hockey boots and distracted myself through sport. I became the youngest player to play for the Hockey First XI, getting elevated from the Under-16s. The team were doing badly and, in my first match, a moment arrived when I was presented with an open goal. All I had to do was push the ball in but instead I took an almighty swing at it and missed the ball completely. I wanted the world to eat me up. But I redeemed myself in the final match of the season when I scored an amazing goal and had an outstanding game – my crimes earlier in the season were forgotten.

In my final year at school, when I was hockey captain, I

broke my leg. It was the first real physical setback I'd ever had. I'd scraped and bruised myself plenty of times in so many rugby and hockey matches but nothing this serious. And it happened during a practice game. I'd scored five goals. The goalkeeper was a huge guy and he got pissed off with me because I was having an absolute stormer. I got through one-on-one with him for another goal, but as I went to round him, he trapped my leg in his. Everyone heard the crack as my leg broke in twelve places. I went from this super-energetic sports dynamo to hobbling around on crutches. I was devastated. I could have diverted my frustrated energy into my studies – but I didn't.

I had made it into the sixth form only to study the hated sciences that my parents thought would lead me smoothly down the path of medicine. A path I had said time and time again that I wouldn't follow. Outside the subjects I studied, sixth-form life was different to being in the lower years. We were nearly as old as some of the teachers and our relationship with most of the masters had shifted as we became more like their equals. We were given responsibilities and I was made house captain of Holman, missing out on head of school to Déj Mahoney. Being house captain brought a lot of work – I had to make sure all the younger boys were in bed and asleep and had to report to the house master every evening; house captains organized the house sports and debating teams, and recruited boys to play rugby, cricket and hockey. I think I adopted a different attitude compared to some of my contemporaries in that I tried to encourage and give younger boys confidence rather than adopt the more aggressive approach that some of the others took. The memory of what it was like to be new and nervous in that environment stuck with me and I wanted to help the younger boys rather than intimidate them.

I managed to avoid the typical teenage vices. There was plenty of opportunity to head to the pub after lights out, and I did go at times, but I never drank in the way that some of the other students did. Some of the masters used to brew their own beer in their houses too (rules were a lot more relaxed then) and as Upper Sixth we'd have a few drinks with them. But I didn't really get into drinking or partying until a few years later, once I had left school. I think this was for two reasons: first, I was such a clean-living sportsman that I didn't want anything to affect my performances on the pitch; and second, I wanted to be house captain. If I had smoked, gone to the pub all the time or done drugs that might have jeopardized my chances. Basically I was a goody two-shoes even though I wasn't exactly the model academic.

I followed through on my promise to my parents and failed two out of my three A levels. In true teenage style, I had written my name at the top of the chemistry and physics exam papers and promptly fallen asleep in protest.

The exam results came through when I was back in Malaysia and my dad was less than happy. Getting a D in biology, O in chemistry (my paper was graded as O-level standard) and F in physics was not what Dad had expected and I was sent back to Epsom to try again. I retook the final year where I could at least play hockey again and came out with slightly better grades (A in biology and Fs in chemistry and physics) – though still not good enough to justify the hefty school fees.

Mum's early death had had a profound effect on me and I was distraught we didn't get to say a proper goodbye when I could tell her how much she had done for me and how much I loved her. Even so, I was determined not to become a doctor, and I didn't try any harder to make my parents' wish come true the second time round.

So I ended school with one A level, many sporting triumphs, the accolade of house captain and an understanding of how to get the best out of people. I loved the camaraderie of boarding school and though some people might have a preconceived idea about what English public schools are like, Epsom wasn't typical in that sense. It didn't feel elitist and I wasn't aware of any class barriers within the school. The staff and pupils were down-to-earth; you became like family and learned to get along with everybody.

My academic record may not have been anything for my parents to brag about, but Epsom taught me a lot about belonging, friendship and teamwork, all of which I've tried to champion in my life in business.

3. The Wilderness Years

Soundtrack: 'Edith and the Kingpin' by Joni Mitchell

When I left Epsom I was nineteen. The only thing I knew for sure was that I didn't want to be a doctor. It's one thing knowing what you *don't* want to do but it's far tougher working out what it is that you actually *do* want to do. Not knowing much about my future plans, I did what a lot of teenagers do nowadays: I went travelling. I refer to this spell as the 'Wilderness Years' because although I learned a lot about myself and about life, I didn't make any kind of progress in my career or impression on the world.

My school friend Midge Finnigan and I settled on the US as our destination. In the 1980s it was a very exciting place, still seen as the land of opportunity where it was relatively easy to get work. I had enough money for the airfare but knew I would have to work while I was travelling around the States, seeing as much of the country as I could along the way. I must have decided at some point that I had been too well-behaved at school because I started to enjoy myself in ways my seventeen-year-old self would not have approved of.

I bought my ticket to New York on TransAmerica Airlines only for them to go bankrupt just before we left. In the end, we flew with Delta and spent the whole flight chatting up the stewardesses and having the first of many parties. We must have made a good impression on the cabin crew because they invited us to a place called Peabody, just beyond Boston. We landed in New York, went to the Howard Johnson Hotel in Jamaica, Queens, unpacked our bags and went out looking for jobs. We worked in New York for about a month and then decided to go up to Boston.

We looked at the map and assumed that Boston wasn't that far, so we rented a 'sub-compact' car – which by UK standards was the size of a Bentley – and headed off. Eight hours later, we arrived. We continually underestimated the scale of everything in America.

I had been working bar jobs in New York, anything I could lay my hands on for a few weeks that would pay the rent and allow me time to go out and experience the city. I loved it. The work situation got even better when we arrived in Boston – I somehow landed a job as the 'third-relief organ player' at Fenway Park, home of the Boston Red Sox. And I did what all Americans do at baseball games: ate mountains of food and drank a lot of beer.

There wasn't a plan but I did have an uncle in Gastonia, North Carolina, so when the partying got a little boring in Boston we headed south on a Greyhound open bus ticket.

North Carolina was where my real US education started, and I began to understand just how segregated the society was. Midge and I were walking around, asking about work, and some of the black people we met asked me, 'Why are you travelling with this white guy?'

And all the white people would ask Midge, 'Why are you travelling with the Indian guy?'

We went to see Marvin Gaye in Charlotte, North Carolina, and Midge was the only white person there. It opened my eyes to what real segregation looks like and made me realize how important it was to be as inclusive of all cultures, races and faiths as possible.

After North Carolina, we worked our way down to Orlando, using the Greyhound pass. We only had a limited number of Greyhound trips and when it got to the last one, we decided we hadn't been far enough west. We looked at the map and decided to head to San Francisco as again, to our naive eyes, it didn't look too far. Three and a half days later we staggered off the coach into the warm Californian sunlight. We worked our way down from San Francisco to Los Angeles and then decided to go back to the UK via Las Vegas, which was the final eye-opener on an extremely revealing trip. I loved Vegas – everything was so cheap, bright, colourful and open. It felt so different to anything I'd seen before.

Midge had decided to travel on to Australia while I went back to London. I left America with fond memories but the divisions I'd experienced within society surprised and unsettled me. The Marvin Gaye concert was the moment that stuck with me for a long time and really shaped my thinking about how people should live and work together. Having witnessed division and people's inward-facing lives in the US at that time, I came back to London with my eyes opened. The world seemed so much bigger than I had imagined and the UK felt so much smaller, and negative in its outlook. In the US, regardless of divisions, success was always celebrated: people flaunted it and were proud of their achievements. In the UK back then people seemed almost embarrassed by success and that confused me. I didn't understand why people did themselves down.

I've always been positive. I think you can make a success of just about anything if you have a positive outlook.

I enjoyed being in London but it wasn't long before Dad cut my partying short and summoned me back to Malaysia. I was booked on a plane home and sitting in Heathrow Terminal 3 waiting for my flight to be called when the dreaded 'flight delayed' announcement came over the tannoy. I walked over to the bar and out of the corner of my eye I saw a cricketer I recognized. It was Max Walker, the Australian bowler, with his signature moustache, sitting at the bar with a few empty glasses in front of him. Max was at the end of a great career for Australia. He had been back-up to the lethal Thomson and Lillee opening attack and had taken a lot of wickets. I was star-struck, but even so I went up and introduced myself. We had a drink, then another and another. I think he must have been telling me that going home wasn't the best idea because the thought started to form in my mind that I should change my ticket to Sydney.

Then things got even more surreal when Billy Joel sat down with us. We stayed in the bar for hours, and at the end of our little party I changed my ticket. Instead of going home I flew to Sydney with Max Walker and went off to meet Midge when I landed. My dad wasn't best pleased, to say the least.

Again, travel opened my eyes. I'd always thought of Australians as being open-minded and positive but I was shocked by most people's unpleasant attitude to the Aboriginals at that time. I heard people in Queensland say that they should be shot. The segregation, the 'them v us'

44

attitude, stuck with me and reinforced the impression I'd
got in the US. I worked on a farm for a few months before
I realized that it was time to decide what I wanted to do
with the rest of my life.

I was twenty when I came back to London. The year out
had taught me a lot, but I hadn't really achieved anything
apart from a new-found ability to party hard. That thought
was starting to bug me. I found myself a job as a waiter in
the Cavendish Hotel in Mayfair which had just recently
become famous thanks to a television series, *The Duchess of
Duke Street*, that was based on the life of the founder of the
hotel, Rosa Lewis. I found the work tough – up at 5.00
a.m., preparing the restaurant, serving the food, dealing
with demanding customers, working through until 10.00
p.m. under the critical eye of the maître d'.

The service industry is brutal – people don't realize how
long the hours are or how tough the physical demands. I
quickly grew to respect and admire the kitchen staff, the
porters and my fellow waiters who came from all over the
world and worked so hard for little reward. The contrast
with my experiences of segregated communities in the US
and Australia could not have been stronger. Here, everyone, regardless of race or colour, pulled together and it
was humbling to see how people still had each other's
backs in such gruelling conditions.

I'm not the world's smartest dresser. If I can get away
with a T-shirt and tracksuit bottoms, that'll do me. At the
Cavendish we had to wear black trousers, a white shirt and
a tie. Not really bothering about my appearance, I set the
tone early on in my career there by arriving one morning

with blood on my collar because I'd cut myself shaving. A fellow waiter stopped me appearing in front of the maître d' in time and gave me a fresh shirt. The next day I was more careful with my shaving but my shirt was still creased from the previous day's work and I was sent home to iron it. My fellow waiters looked out for me but I think I tried their patience a lot. Life in the Cavendish was hard for everyone – the hours were back-breakingly long, the pay horrendous and the working conditions brutal. But I'll never forget the camaraderie.

I realized how much better it is to embrace everyone regardless of how rich or poor they are, what colour skin they have, what religion they follow. I'll happily talk to anyone and treat them equally – I think it is my one real strength.

As well as learning about fairness, the Cavendish also showed me what the future looked like without a proper education. And that was grim. So I decided to retake my A levels, choosing subjects that I actually wanted to study this time: history and economics. My aunt lived in Birmingham and I arranged to go and stay with her while I went to a cheap crammer school in the city. She was initially happy to see me but I still liked to party, so she threw me out after a couple of months because I was a distraction to her own teenage kids. Forever the disruptor!

This was when I really started to understand what life was about. I got a bedsit in School Road, Moseley, and for the first time I was alone and had to look after myself. It was a revelation. It didn't stop me partying but it did make me appreciate how much it takes to hold everything together: feeding yourself, keeping everything clean, making money last and all the countless other things you only learn when you have to fend for yourself. I started to have more of an understanding of my dad's frugal approach to life.

This time I achieved grades that were good enough to get me a place studying accountancy at university in London. My dad was proud that I'd finally achieved something academically – it wasn't much but it was a step in the right direction. However, things didn't go quite the way my dad thought they would. There's a pub on the corner of Warrington Crescent and Randolph Avenue in Maida Vale and in front of it is a turfed-over roundabout which sits like a green island in the middle of a tarmac sea. The first thing that comes to mind when I think about university is that roundabout. We seemed to spend a lot of time in that pub and that's probably the reason why my memory of that time is so blurry. I don't think the university saw much of me until I took my finals.

Alongside my pub activities, I looked to educate myself further in the ways of the world through the various university societies rather than dwell on the intricacies of double-entry bookkeeping. During Freshers' Week I toured the groups and societies in the main hall and ended up in front of the Malaysia–Singapore Society table.

A guy looked up.

'Hi. Are you Malaysian? You should join us. We do loads of events that put us in touch with home.'

I looked at him with a slightly confused expression and said, 'Why would I want to do that? I know all about Malaysia and Singapore, I'm interested in the rest of the world . . .' and wandered off. I think they were a bit pissed

47

off but to me it made absolutely no sense to join a group of people from the same country. Instead I joined the Brazilian Society and had a better time discovering things about a part of the world I hadn't visited, where football was a religion.

I was living in Maida Vale, hanging out with a big group of friends – some from Epsom and others I'd met in London or who were friends of friends – and the university didn't seem that bothered about whether I went to lectures or not. Party time. I'd head off to Calais for the day to buy wine and beer for parties or go to Paris to see bands. I remember seeing the Police at an open-air concert where the French crowd pelted the support band, A Flock of Seagulls, with mud. I thought the band were pretty good – it was just the French being impatient.

Sometimes I'd spend the day at Lord's, the home of cricket, not only to watch the match but also because the bar was open all day.

Another close school friend, Mick McBryde, was renting his brother's flat in Ladbroke Gardens, Notting Hill, and I seemed to spend a huge amount of time there in 1984–5. Mick still has the Visitors' Book and there are many pages with my name scrawled on; I must have virtually lived there. Mick and I would go to local parties or just hang out playing Monopoly. I was always the racing car, of course, and once I beat him twice in an hour. As we sat there late into the night, we'd talk about all the business ideas we had and we'd listen to music – Joni Mitchell's album *The Hissing of Summer Lawns* was our favourite, and one track, 'Edith and the Kingpin', must have worn out, we played it so much. (Almost twenty years later, Joni

Mitchell came out to Malaysia and I mentioned that Mick and I used to listen to that song constantly. She was kind enough to sign a copy of her new CD for Mick, saying she hoped it brought back happy memories.)

At the time Mick and I were hanging out in Ladbroke Gardens, I had moved to the Uxbridge Road, within a stone's throw of Loftus Road, QPR's ground. Mick got a temp job pulling pints at the Loftus Road bar and was serving the night I went to see Barry McGuigan take on the legendary Eusebio Pedroza in June 1985. It was an epic fight. McGuigan got a points decision after fifteen rounds and it was to be the best night of his fighting career. It was also my introduction to what would become my sporting home in London thirty years later.

The great thing about London is that it offered a party every night if you wanted to go out and I usually did. We'd often end up in the basement of a Russian restaurant called Borshtch 'n' Tears in Knightsbridge, drinking until the early hours with whoever had made it that far into the night.

As you can guess, the academic aspect of university still didn't interest me at all, but business did. Like every other student, I was paying rent and thought it was a rip-off, but unlike most students I decided to do something about it. The challenge I set myself was to buy a house. I had no salary so getting a mortgage looked impossible. Nevertheless, I wrote to and called hundreds of financial advisors – and I mean hundreds – but they all either laughed at me or flat-out refused. I kept going, working my way through the telephone directory, following up on leads from friends or hitting the streets and going into offices on spec. Time and again advisors told me it was impossible and I should give up but I wouldn't do it. Having said that, even I was starting to doubt if I could pull it off when I found my luck in an Irish Life broker on Streatham High Road. If you've never been to Streatham – and particularly if you never saw it in the eighties – you'll have trouble understanding just how unlikely it was that I'd have a chance of a deal there. But I did. I hit it off with the broker straight away – perhaps he liked the glint in my eye and the off-the-wall request – and he offered me a deal. I had explained that I was being financed by my dad and that I wanted to use that as my proof of income. Somehow he managed to swing it. I got a £26,000 mortgage and bought a house in Colney Hatch Lane, Muswell Hill. I consider that my first proper business deal.

Part of getting that deal was down to showmanship, and wanting to prove my original bank wrong. I had been with NatWest bank since my Epsom days but had only picked them because they sponsored cricket (a branding lesson which wasn't lost on me when it came to AirAsia).

They were one of the first banks I approached for a mortgage but the bank manager just laughed at me. I don't necessarily blame him now but I was really angry and decided that if they didn't want my business I'd take it somewhere else. I was told that Coutts was the most prestigious bank in England so, wanting to show my importance to the world and prove a point, I tracked down the nearest branch of Coutts to the university. I'd heard that it was almost impossible to get an account if your family hadn't banked with them before or if you weren't a member of the Royal Family – they are the Queen's bankers after all.

A week after I'd decided NatWest had failed the test, I walked to the Fleet Street branch of Coutts. There was a doorman stationed outside – a Coutts tradition – and I felt I had to make my case to him before I was allowed in. Then, inside the wood-panelled office, I sat in front of an intimidating elderly man in a dark grey suit and tails, the epitome of a banker. I told him about all of the business ideas Mick and I had dreamed up over the years in Notting Hill. I must have come across as determined because I ended up with a Coutts bank account and, most importantly, a chequebook. In the eighties, Coutts' chequebooks were bigger than any other bank's, which always impressed people. When I got to Streatham, I pulled out the chequebook and I could see the broker's expression change: this guy is a player, it said. So by the time I was twenty, I owned my own home. I have been buying and selling property regularly ever since.

At some point over the course of the three years, I must have turned up at university because I remember sitting my finals and scraping a pass grade. Once again, my dad was getting anxious back in Malaysia. He had sold the house we grew up in, in part to finance my studies, and, by now frustrated with me, issued an ultimatum.

'Anthony, either you study to qualify as an accountant or you come home and work in Kuala Lumpur. I won't continue to fund you to do nothing.'

That did the trick. I immediately enrolled to study accountancy at the London School of Accountancy (LSA) on Marylebone Road. To become an accountant I had to pass a number of exams. But at least it would mean a guaranteed job; accountants are always in demand. I didn't take my studies seriously there either but somehow I managed to pass what were called my Level 2 exams. I then decided to go for my Level 3, which would put me in a better position for a job, so I signed up to the Emile Woolf School. The lectures were the first (and last) in my higher education career that I enjoyed – possibly because I could see how the skills and knowledge I was acquiring might be used in the real world. I instinctively understood the financial management modules in particular.

Even so, I found myself with a month to go before my Level 3 exams in a blind sweat. If I didn't pass I'd be going back in shame to Kuala Lumpur, leaving my London life behind for ever. I locked myself away at the University of London's Senate House Library and worked from 9.00 in the morning until it closed. Three months later, I was in my aunt's house in Aldermaston when the results came through. I was so nervous that I ran to the bottom of the garden to open the envelope alone.

PASS

PASS

PASS

PASS

I was elated. I had qualified as an accountant: the first time I'd achieved anything academically.

Dad was chuffed too when I told him the news – he hadn't thought much of my degree, but *this* was an achievement. The next stop was to enter the world of work.

I applied for jobs at small companies, got several offers and settled on an accounting firm called Brewers. They loved me, but I hated it. It was the worst job I've ever had.

From the moment I arrived I could see my life stretching ahead like one long boring prison sentence. I was the junior auditor and basically my job was to photocopy. The hardest part of it was filling out the timesheets because you had to account for every fifteen minutes of your day – most of the time I did nothing so it was a challenge to think of things to write. Within a few weeks I came to the decision that I would look for an accountancy job in the music industry. I wrote to every record company asking about positions there and every single one rejected me.

I persevered – as I always do – and eventually an ad appeared in the newspaper for a job as a financial manager at Virgin Television. I applied, thinking that it was my last shot. When the letter arrived inviting me for an interview I felt that my life was at last about to get better.

By this time, at the end of 1987, I was married, I owned a house which I was renting out and I was a qualified accountant, a career that wouldn't bring disgrace to my family. My now ex-wife and I had met during my party years and settled down quickly in Muswell Hill, but in order to respect her privacy I won't go into further details.

So my Wilderness Years were the making of me. Epsom had been character-building but I was living in a protected environment – food, shelter and money were all things that I didn't really need to worry about. Leaving school and striking out without support taught me some fundamentals about the world and how I wanted to live my life. I learned that if you want something, you have to keep at it until you succeed. I'd never have got the mortgage if I hadn't chased down every lead and written to every broker I could find until I met the guy at Irish Life. Sometimes you have to put on a bit of a show – or in this case, a Coutts account – if you want to reach something that's meant to be beyond you. I also grasped that I'm a very hands-on learner. Being told something in a dry, academic situation doesn't appeal to me. I've got to see how it works and the effect it has in the real world before I fully understand it.

I also learned about the importance of listening and talking to people with genuine interest. You could drop me anywhere in the world and I'd immediately start chatting to anybody and everybody around me.

In business, and in life, getting on with people is about making them feel comfortable and finding common ground. Knowing something about their culture helps a lot and it's a shame too many businesses embrace only their own national culture and are narrow-minded in their outlook. Business is global now. My travels went a long way to ready me for business adventures still to come.

4. My Life in Music

Soundtrack: 'Thank You for the Music' by ABBA

The interview at Virgin was very short.

'Why do you think you're suitable for this job?'

I talked about my love of music, how I was impressed by Richard Branson's approach to business and the success of Virgin overall, but I had nothing to point to that I had achieved that would make them think I could add anything to the job or the company.

'Well, that's all very well, Mr Fernandes, but what experience do you have that makes you qualified to work here?'

That was the problem, I didn't. I left the interview crushed. This had been my one chance to get close to the music business and I'd messed it up. A lifetime of work at Brewers stretched before me. As I stood in the foyer deciding what to do, Richard Branson walked in. It was a true *Sliding Doors* moment – my life could take one of two directions depending on how I dealt with this. I realized I could be a pussy, smile at him and walk on, or I could actually say something to him that would get his attention and make him interested in me. So I said, 'Hey, Richard, I'm from Malaysia.'

That was enough of a hook for him to try to find out more.

'Why are you here?'

'Came for a job but I messed the interview up.'

'Oh.' He looked me up and down. 'Let's have a coffee.'

It's hard to overestimate the importance of that moment on the rest of my life.

Since then, one of my guiding principles has been that if you see a chance, a flicker of an opportunity, you have to take it. If nothing comes of it you haven't lost anything; but you might just change your life if you have a go. If I hadn't stopped Richard that day I'd never have got into the music business, and who knows what path I would have taken.

Over coffee we chatted about Malaysia, my family, my passion for music and about what I wanted to do with my life. Once again all those fantasy businesses I'd dreamed up with Mick McBryde proved useful.

At the end of twenty minutes, Richard said: 'There's something about you. I'll talk to the head of department and you can have another interview.' He was as good as his word and I found myself working at Virgin TV a month later.

Richard Branson's approach impressed me. That style of going with your gut – thinking that as long as someone fits the culture, they'll find a role – is something I have followed in business.

At Virgin Television I was given the job of accountant. Looking back, Virgin was definitely ahead of its time. There were three parts to the TV arm: a post-production company (called 525 – where I ended up working), a design company and Music Box, a competitor to MTV that changed into something called Super Channel, a satellite channel intended to compete against Sky (and co-owned with a lot of the ITV companies); but while the idea was visionary, the technology lagged so far behind that you'd have needed a satellite dish as big as a house to receive it. I think it was the first company to have CGI graphics as well – again, the computer was as big as a block of flats but the idea was inspired.

I loved the culture at Virgin – so refreshing after the stuffiness of Brewers. No one gave a damn what I looked like or when I turned up to work. It was friendly and inclusive, and the pace was laid-back but creative. After six months I was spotted by the head of 525 and moved there as financial manager. The atmosphere was so chilled that 525's cash book had 'marijuana' as an entry, and the balance sheet didn't balance! I'm not sure if the two were connected.

This was a radical culture for the eighties, even if now it seems sane and rational. There was also the inspiring 'screw it, let's do it' approach to innovation. Even today I come across companies that get so bogged down in spreadsheets, projections and forecasts, they sap the life out of new projects or initiatives – I call it 'analysis paralysis'. But often if it feels right, it *is* right . . . no amount of Excel-pounding will get you to a better decision. Virgin certainly planted the seed of that approach and attitude all those years ago.

At first I couldn't make head or tail of the books; I would ring up my girlfriend and ask her questions about what numbers should go where. Then, one day, everything clicked. I started on a full clean-up of the accounts, which I enjoyed – much to my surprise.

I had been there two years when Richard announced that he was interested in starting an airline. And, though it makes us both laugh now, I thought he'd lost it. I was convinced he was going to sell the music business to finance it, which I would have hated. So I started to look around for another job – although my role in the Virgin Group was on the television side, I was still hoping to work in the music business eventually. If Virgin sold its music business then I would be even further away from my dream career.

I was skimming the jobs in *The Times* one morning on my way to work. It was busy on the tube and I hadn't been able to open the newspaper fully because there were too many people wedged around me. I was about to turn to the sports section when I saw the Warner Music logo. Warner was the epicentre of the music business as far as I was concerned. So many of my most-played records came from Warner – Chaka Khan, Fleetwood Mac, Joni Mitchell, Madonna and Prince. I also knew a bit about Steve Ross, the CEO for many years. His leadership style – a hands-off approach that devolved responsibility down the ranks to people who knew the job inside out – was ahead of its time. He was also a visionary within TV, creating channels that served a particular interest and audience, MTV, Nickelodeon, etc. Finally, industry legends like Mo Ostin and Ahmet Ertegun, who'd found and nurtured so much musical talent, were embedded within Warner. Between them they had provided the soundtrack to my life so far, including Ray Charles and all the old Atlantic soul records. Warner probably contributed 75 per cent of my music collection. I got off the tube at the next stop to study the advert.

The role was financial analyst in the Warner International division – a step down from the financial manager position at Virgin, but I didn't care. I got an interview through a headhunter and found myself sitting in front of a man called Don Sweeney, who was the assistant financial controller for Warner Worldwide in their Baker Street offices. The job was to write reports on the financial performance of each country in your allotted territory.

I celebrated big style when I was offered the job. I was still young – twenty-six or so – and had made it into the music business. Granted, I was in finance rather than A&R; but I've always believed that if you want to work in a particular industry you just need to get your foot in the door. It doesn't matter about the specific job because once you're on the inside you can figure your way forward from a much stronger position. Something, by the way, I've always encouraged in AirAsia.

From day one I got really stuck into it. The countries in my portfolio were Scandinavia, Italy and Germany. I read my predecessor's reports and had a look at what some of the other analysts were doing and it struck me that they were just parroting the obvious – putting into words what the numbers were already showing. There was no real analysis, just commentary. So I started to dig into the stories behind the numbers. I'd fly out to Stockholm or Rome and try to understand what was going on in the local market so that the reports would be more useful.

The perks were fantastic. I would drop into the marketing department and walk away with CDs that hadn't even been released yet; my music collection was growing faster than ever. And tracks were always playing in the office so it was a perfect place for me to be.

But the work I was actually paid to do – writing these

pointless reports – was driving me mad. Even with the extra information and insight I was getting from people 'on the front line', the reports looked like something from the sixties. I went to my boss and asked whether I could change the format and style, knowing it was a big risk. He was adamant that I shouldn't; it was the way it had always been done and it was how the president wanted to see the numbers presented and analysed. I still thought it was backward.

I bought a copy of Harvard Graphics spreadsheet software, added graphs and charts to my report, and included extra local market analysis and insights. I sent it out late one evening, thinking that I'd be sacked as soon as my boss saw it. I loved being in the music business but, frankly, my day-to-day job sucked. So I figured I had nothing to lose in trying something different.

The next day I got into the office and saw my whole department crowded around one computer staring at the screen. I approached and realized they were looking at my report. I thought, 'OK, that really is it. I'd better collect my things and leave.' I asked why they were all looking at it.

'The chairman says it's the best he's ever seen,' one said.

Stephen Shrimpton – number two at Warner Music at the time – asked to see me. Stephen was already a legend at Warner and he rose to become chairman and CEO of Warner International; he was also an intimidating guy. He was known to have a temper and would scream, shout and throw things at people, in the way that senior people could get away with back then. But Stephen took a real liking to me.

Some actions in your career either give you a leg up or hold you back; sending out that report was a moment when I got a massive boost.

Just before I had sent the report I'd had a holiday in Malaysia. While I was there I had dropped in on the CEO of Warner Malaysia, an Austrian guy, Günther Zeiter. When we met we'd talked about the possibility of my returning to Malaysia to help out there. So when I saw Stephen we talked about Malaysia and he suggested that one day I could go back there as general manager. Two years later he mentioned it again and I leapt at the chance – I didn't bother to ask about the 'package', I just said 'yes'. There are moments when you've got to seize the opportunity presented to you and Stephen wasn't someone, I guessed, who'd be impressed by hesitation. So I went for it and it changed my life.

My then wife and I packed up and travelled to Malaysia in style – I bought first-class round-the-world tickets with Continental Airlines. We flew to New York, Florida, San Francisco and then to Malaysia. It was an emotional departure from Gatwick because I'd always thought I'd end up living in England permanently – I'd felt at home there since a few weeks into my first term at Epsom. I had so enjoyed the English way of life and sense of humour; my friends even called me 'The Brown Englishman' because I had adopted so many of their ways.

Soon after we landed in Malaysia, the reality of my new job and situation hit me. After living and working in London, Kuala Lumpur felt small, provincial and isolated – certainly not the connected city it is now. I was an accountant by training, not a music industry person, and knew absolutely nothing about the Malaysian or South East Asian music scenes. The final straw as far as my new colleagues were concerned was that I had never even been a manager in my professional career. My appointment must have looked strange from the outside. I learned early on that the staff were planning to boycott me because they thought I was some young punk who knew nothing. They weren't completely wrong – I was only twenty-eight, after all.

I managed to turn their attitudes around when I started working because I was friendly and got on with people on a personal level. I also changed the way we ran things, making everyone more accountable and giving them more autonomy to get on with their jobs. That's been my leadership style ever since – broadly trusting people to get on with the job they're employed to do. It has sometimes caused me grief but I prefer to work on the basis that good people know what they're doing. I used the 'walkaround' management style and really listened to what people had to say; I made sure that I understood what everyone did and I think I brought a passion and a belief into what we were doing. Getting the books in order and making sure the processes of distribution were smooth helped with the bottom line, but energy was the most important change I made.

Operationally, I felt comfortable, but as far as the local music was concerned, I had a lot to learn. So I started listening; I'd get the A&R man, Nasser Abdul Kassim, to bring me Malaysian music, he'd put on a tape and we'd decide whether to sign the artist or not. I felt that the scene at the time was actually quite boring and safe, and that there had to be better new music out there than what we were producing and distributing. Our catalogue was selling but it didn't feel exciting to me, despite what I told the staff.

I was thinking that the whole music scene in Malaysia was due a shake-up. Then one day a man called Roslan Aziz walked into my office. Roslan is a legend – as a producer, musician and recording artist, he's been behind so much of Malaysia's greatest music. Nasser had already signed him but Roslan had come in to give us a cassette of his new stuff to listen to. I think he thought I was fresh meat and that he might be able to get a load of cash out of me. But from the moment the music started, I was blown away. The quality was unique – a kind of *Graceland* meets Malay pop. It was smart music and it was Malaysian, which made a huge difference. I wanted to discover local talent and here it was, outstanding and staring me in the face. I genuinely thought that what I heard could break the world markct. (Sadly, it never quite did – for it to work globally that kind of music needed a Western face or to be included on a film soundtrack. We never got those breaks but it was still exciting music.)

Though he had a reputation as being a bit difficult, slow and meticulous in the studio, Roslan also owned a record label called RAP (Roslan Aziz Productions) with his wife, Sheila Majid, Zainal Abidin and a few others. I thought I'd unearthed a treasure trove of great Malaysian music in his label and decided to buy it for Warner Music. On the other side of the negotiating table as we fleshed out the deal was RAP's finance man, Kamarudin Meranun Din, who drove a hard bargain.

In the end, we paid a lot and Roslan's reputation for being slow and a perfectionist was well justified. The purchase turned out to be one of my biggest mistakes during my time at Warner. We only made three albums with them and none of them was commercial enough. The music was great but way too complex for the market and consequently they never sold, despite the marketing money we threw at them. Albums took for ever to produce so we never really captured the essence of what RAP was. It wasn't all Roslan's fault, though. I didn't manage the talent closely enough, leaving them to their own devices. It's a flaw of mine that when I see talented people I trust them to get on. Sometimes I trust too much. It was the same at QPR for the first few seasons. These days I can recognize when things are going off the rails earlier – it's taken me two attempts but I'm more alert to it now.

One great thing that came out of the deal was meeting Din. I said to him, 'Next time we do a deal I want you on my side of the table.' And that was the start of one of the most important relationships of my life.

The pace of change at Warner Malaysia was so fast that I don't think I had a moment to take a breath; after six months Stephen Shrimpton and some of the other bosses came over to visit and see our progress. We were sitting in a conference room doing our presentations about the business and reviewing which albums and artists we'd be taking on in the next season. After one particularly long discussion during which I'd argued for an artist and got reluctant approval from everyone, Stephen turned to me and said, 'You're running everything, you might as well be CEO.'

Günther Zeiter, the then-CEO of Warner Malaysia, was in the room at the time – Americans can be blunt that way. But a week later they fired Günther after Ella 'The Queen of Rock' (Ratu Rock), one of Malaysia's biggest artists, walked free to EMI. Whoever had drawn up the contract had forgotten to put in what's called the Option Clause which allowed us first refusal on her next album. It was one of the biggest disasters to hit the company and the final straw for Günther. So at the age of twenty-eight I took over as CEO of Warner Malaysia.

Since moving back to Kuala Lumpur, we'd spent much more time together as a family. My daughter, Steph, had just been born, so most weekends we'd go to Dad's for lunch or just hang out with him and my sister. It was a wonderful time and I'm grateful to have had it – particularly after Mum had been taken away so cruelly.

But just as I was starting to really enjoy life back in Malaysia, with my career taking off and personally feeling at home again, Dad grew ill and died of emphysema. Despite the fact that he smoked incessantly – as did virtually all his generation – it still came as a shock. Like Mum, he was taken too early, but at least I think he died a happy man. Although he didn't give me any credit for my achievements, I think he was pleased I was finally making a success of my family and career. Of course, he never told me that directly, but I did hear it through his friends.

When Mum died, I had turned to sport to channel my grief; this time I focused on signing artists. I went on a band acquisition spree and ran the whole company really aggressively, battling hard for musicians we wanted and negotiating tough contracts to make sure we got the best deals.

In 1993, Nasser, my A&R man, brought a religious band to me. They were called Raihan – five guys who sang together with minimal backing. As soon as I heard them, I wanted them on our books. So much Malaysian music at the time was minor chords, sickly sweet love songs and sad ballads, but Raihan had a purity about their voices and an energy in their harmonies that sang to me. The five men wore green shirts and make-up. I was hooked.

They lived in an Al-Arqam commune in Kuala Lumpur. Al-Arqam was a controversial, Islamic movement which was led by a charismatic leader called Ashaari Mohammad. The commune itself was advanced and self-sustaining as far as food, water, education and social structures were concerned, but there were strong rumours that it was being watched closely by the government. When we arrived I got a bit freaked out by the whole scene and decided reluctantly that signing them wasn't worth the risk. Sure enough, in October 1994 the sect was banned by the Malaysian government.

A year later, after the ban, Raihan came back with their producer, Farihin Abdul Fattah. Still with their make-up on but this time in white. And I told Nasser to sign them straight away despite the fact that no one else in the company believed in them. Religious music wasn't touched by any of the major labels or distributors so it was a punt into the unknown. But we got behind the album, called *Puji-Pujian*, spent money on videos, and it exploded. The first shipment, when it was released in 1996, was 500 units and it has gone on to sell 3.5 million worldwide. It was huge.

A bonus was the way the music crossed racial, religious and cultural boundaries. In Malaysia at the time the Chinese bought Chinese music, Malays bought Malay, and so on. This was the first time that the same music was being listened to by the whole country and it was the first time that you saw Malay, Chinese and Indians at the same concerts. Raihan broke that mould.

For the second Raihan album, I got Yusuf Islam (Cat Stevens) in to collaborate and they recorded a couple of songs together in London. He'd seen Raihan when he was in Malaysia and had loved the fact they promoted Islam through their music. We broke Raihan internationally and they've been touring ever since. And they're great – even though they became superstars of the Islamic world, they remained humble, always staying behind to sign autographs and help us clean up after gigs or stack chairs after events. Fame and success didn't change them. They were all-round good guys.

On the back of Raihan, we created a market for the religious music that was so popular in the region by packaging it in a commercial way. It was highly profitable for us and funded lots of the riskier punts I took.

Once we brought religious music into the mainstream with Raihan, other local music styles followed. There was a genre called 'Dangdut', which is a strange mix of Hindustani, Arabic and Malay musical traditions. It had been seen as 'low-class' music and hadn't had backing by a major label. But I wasn't interested in what class it was; the only thing that mattered to me was if there was a market for it and whether it could be profitable. It turns out that the answer to both questions was a very big 'yes'. We packaged Dangdut music up in a way that appealed to its core audience and knocked out compilation albums and CDs as quickly as we could. We put all our efforts into pushing the music and shifted good numbers in Indonesia and Malaysia. This was not an affluent market so we put on a free concert at the Johor Bahru stadium in southern Malaysia. I compared this kind of music to the 'Macarena' and the 'Lambada', and hoped that it would be picked up globally.

Although I was implementing such initiatives for Warner, the music industry as a whole in the South East Asian region was still quite backward. Having seen the way the European and US record labels worked, I set about creating superstructures for the industry: charts, an academy and the Recording Industry Association of Malaysia (RIM). I figured that it's not just about marketing your own products, it's about creating a market if one doesn't already exist. Professionalizing the industry as well as your own company always yields dividends – the better the standards in the industry as a whole, the more growth you can generate.

Part of that industry-wide approach was taking on piracy, which was killing the business in Asia. There was a report by the International Federation of Phonogram and Videogram Producers published in 1989 which said that 95 per cent of all the tapes and cassettes sold in Bangkok were pirated. Apparently the only non-pirated cassettes available were collections of jazz songs written or performed by the King of Thailand, Bhumibol Adulyadej, mainly because it was a criminal offence to use the king's name in any context other than a respectful one. In Malaysia, piracy was running at 50 per cent. Millions of dollars were being lost each year to pirates.

The only way of tackling it was to pay a visit to the gangsters who were running these operations. So I did. We worked with the police to try to shut the operations down. Often late at night, Datuk Pahamin Ab Rajab, the secretary-general of the Malaysian Domestic Trade and Consumer Affairs Ministry, and I would find ourselves sitting in the back of a police truck with forty armed officers waiting for the command to go and raid a warehouse. These ramshackle buildings in industrial parks in Kuala Lumpur were the place where CDs were copied and then shipped out to be sold on the streets. Of course, we usually caught the little guys, the minnows of the operation, but I felt it was important to do something rather than just let it happen and see our profits and our artists suffer. As a leader I thought it was important to be on the front line fighting for the causes I believed in, no matter how dangerous it might be.

As well as finding, nurturing and releasing great local talent, we were also always on the lookout for international stars. We were fed a diet of Western bands that we had to take in and distribute as part of being in the Warner Group but that never felt as satisfying as finding something that Warner hadn't picked up already. The Corrs were one of those bands whose success gave me real pleasure. Two good friends, the legendary producer David Foster and Brian Avnet, artist manager, gave me their CD *Talk on Corners* in 1997. I loved it and played it to the Warner Asia team. At the time, two guys from EMI had just arrived in the company, Calvin Wong, who was head of regional marketing and Lachie Rutherford, who was president of the Asia region. Calvin was talented but liked to disagree with everything I said; he said he couldn't see how it would work in Asia and refused to get behind it.

I went ahead and did the deal anyway. I loved their story – four talented siblings (including three beautiful sisters) from Ireland who sang melodies and harmonies and had learned to play together at their aunt's pub in Dundalk, County Louth. They'd appeared in the film *The Commitments* but their break had really come when the US ambassador had them play at the 1994 World Cup in Boston.

They were still unknown in Asia but we were getting creative with marketing and publicity so we invited them over to Kuala Lumpur to play the closing ceremony of the Commonwealth Games in September 1998. That was a good incentive but I added a white lie to convince them: I said they'd be introduced to the Queen. Although that nearly happened, I couldn't quite pull it off so they were fed up with me for a while. But on the back of the Commonwealth Games they had one of the biggest-selling albums of the year. I'd gone out on a limb and it had paid off.

The pace at which we were signing new artists and releasing new albums was breathtaking, and in the end it caught up with us. We had a few bad years in the late nineties where we pushed out huge quantities of too many artists – old and new – but they just wouldn't move, so we had to bring the stock back.

At that point, Stephen Shrimpton came to see me and said, 'Slow down! You're too much like a man in a hurry. There's time; use it.'

I took his advice. I slashed our lists and made the company refocus on its core artists rather than trying to do too much. The business was picking up again and I was getting my reputation back as a bit of a star. Since then the accusation of being 'a man in a hurry' is one that has been applied to me a few times and I know I can be guilty of it. There's a temptation when things are going well to overstretch and let your attention drift from doing your main job and executing the most important duties well.

I was also distracted by the desire to keep moving up the ladder. I'd shot through the upper ranks of Warner and had my eyes on being made head of the South East Asian region. Ambition drove that but I could also see the value of creating a coordinated South East Asian market even then. Stephen Shrimpton had been fielding my increasingly urgent messages saying that I wanted the promotion but he had kept putting a decision off until the top echelons of management in Asia had remained stable for a while. There had been a lot of movement in and out of the boardroom which had caused problems and he wanted a period of calm before acting on my behalf.

Calvin Wong and Lachie Rutherford had been brought in from EMI to provide that stability but they didn't seem to like me for whatever reason, and I felt they were trying to ease me out. Often when a new top-tier team come in they want to put their own people in place. That said, I did technically get my promotion in 1999 but it felt like more of a holding tactic than anything else. Neither Calvin nor Lachie thought I fitted the bill but gave me the job while they decided what to do with me.

My new job didn't really give me any new scope to

develop my ideas: I wanted to create a structure that properly engaged with the South East Asian region but my new bosses weren't supportive, and I was too senior to do a lot of the work I'd loved doing before. The writing was on the wall, but there was one final album to make.

One of our biggest singing stars was S. M. Salim – think Frank Sinatra levels of fame in Malaysia. He'd been with Warner for many years but his sales had been slumping until I had arrived; I got him to record a song with Zainal Abidin in 1992 which became a lasting hit. He then told us he'd like to make a farewell album. Nasser and I thought it was a great idea; we teamed him up with the Malaysian Philharmonic Orchestra, which was Prime Minister Mahathir's pet project, and persuaded Siti Nurhaliza to join him (if Salim is the Frank Sinatra of Malaysia, Siti is the Celine Dion or Mariah Carey). A live album that crossed genres so ambitiously had never before been attempted; the costs were high but it was a runaway success and ultimately earned Warner, the orchestra and the artists a lot of money. The Prime Minister went to the concert and on the back of it granted S. M. Salim a Tan Sri-ship, a high honour. He was so proud – and I was too, as it was a high point of my music career. This album was recorded in January 2001, and it was the last one I worked on before leaving Warner in May.

It had been a long time coming. My frustrations with a stalled career, my South East Asian ambitions thwarted and the slow pace of change in a big corporation all contributed to my departure but what pushed me over the edge was the industry's reaction to digital downloading. The attitude was either to bury their collective head in the sand or to belittle it. My view was that the technology was here to stay, so you couldn't try to stop it – instead you had to work with it and try to reap the benefits. It was like when the car came along and everyone in the delivery business said that they'd keep using horses. I felt we should be taking on this new way of listening to music, exploring its potential and making the most out of it instead of leaving it to the Napsters of this world. The complacent industry reaction frustrated me enormously.

Today I am always keeping an eye out for such moments – edgy innovations that point to seismic shifts. Whenever I sense AirAsia or any of my other businesses is becoming heavy-footed and can't anticipate or respond quickly to new technology, I worry. Business is about agility and being able to move without being weighed down by processes, committees and working groups. There are too many examples of successful companies being brought down by their lack of awareness or nimbleness when technology or the market changes – look at Kodak or Nokia and a lot of retail outlets who didn't embrace changes in technology which threatened their traditional products. In business you have to be aware of these developments and you have to respond.

Leaving Warner was the right thing to do not only because the industry refused to innovate but also because I was starting to lose interest, and my own performance started to falter because of it. I've always tried to 'be the best, do the max' but I reached a point where I couldn't do anything more for the industry even in the position I was in. This was problematic for me because I'm a strong believer that you should earn and deserve your salary every single day. It was one of the things that confused me when I took over QPR and saw players who were earning a fortune but weren't giving everything to the game. I personally don't understand how anyone can draw a salary and not fully commit to their job. When my performance was dipping because I didn't believe in what I was doing, I knew I had to go.

I sat down with the senior team at Warner in early 2001 and we agreed a severance package. I negotiated with them to let me keep my office space in the Warner building in MUI Plaza, Kuala Lumpur, along with my brilliant assistant, Kim, and my company car. I thought my office would be useful to retain for whatever new adventure lay ahead; from their side, they realized there were a lot of loose ends to tie up, so they felt it would be to everyone's advantage that I kept it.

Though I loved my time in the music industry, I felt good about leaving Warner. Along the way I'd met some great people, including Din, Kathleen Tan, who ran Warner Singapore after joining as regional head of marketing, Tassapon Bijleveld, who was CEO of Warner Thailand, Sendjaja Widjaja in Indonesia, Marianne 'Maan' Hontiveros in the Philippines and many others. We had farewell parties in each of the countries, and at each they made sure that they played two songs: 'Thank You for the Music' by ABBA and 'I Believe I Can Fly' by R. Kelly. One looking back and one forward. When I made my farewell speech in Indonesia, I looked forward and said that one day they'd all work for me again. Turns out I was right.

The final meeting with Warner was in New York and, when it was over, I flew to London. I didn't really have a clue what to do. I didn't think I had the balls to become an entrepreneur but I'd asked around half-heartedly in the music business and there weren't any openings that tempted me. When I first landed my job at Virgin and then at Warner, I had thought I'd die working in the music business because I loved it so much, but now it felt a bit stale and I sensed there were other things I could do. I just had to find them.

When I returned to London, I was at a loose end. One afternoon in February 2001 I made my way to the Spaniards Inn, a famous old pub on the edge of Hampstead Heath. I was sitting there nursing a sparkling water when I saw Stelios pop up on television. I knew he was the founder of easyJet, the orange-branded low-cost airline that was growing so quickly in the UK. As he was being interviewed, I leaned in closer.

5. Daring to Dream

Soundtrack: 'I Believe I Can Fly' by R. Kelly

A few things came together in my mind in that pub, when I was listening to Stelios speak. I loved aeroplanes, airports and the aviation business. I was great at marketing and promotion. There were no low-cost airlines that I knew of operating in Asia.

I had to see for myself. That very afternoon I jumped on a bus at Hampstead to Brent Cross shopping centre, and there I made a connection with a 757 Green Line coach to Luton Airport – the same coach company that delivered me to Epsom, and that Charlie Hunt and I used to take to Heathrow twenty years before.

I walked into the terminal and was blown away. It felt like the entire airport was easyJet branded – orange was everywhere. Passengers flying off to Barcelona for £8 or Paris for £6 looked so happy. The whole operation was impressive, from the blanket branding of the airport to the simplicity of the offer.

I decided I was going to start an airline. The words I'd spoken to my mum on the phone all those years ago came back to me: I was going to make it affordable to fly from Kuala Lumpur to London. Before I left Luton I bought a Handycam and filmed everything so I could remember every detail of the operation, from the easyJet branding at the entrance, to the airport building, to the uniforms of the check-in staff. I loved the overwhelming brand feel that passengers got from the airport.

As it happened, I got a call from Din soon after. He was stuck in some remote place on the Iraq–Turkey border and needed help getting a hotel room and a flight back. We'd kept in touch throughout my Warner days and I got him good corporate rates for travel. When he called, I asked him what he thought about setting up an airline. He sounded enthusiastic but had a more pressing concern.

'Sure, sounds great. Now can you get me that deal on the hotel room?' Din is never one to pass up the chance for a discount.

I flew back to Malaysia and Din and I met to discuss the basic plan, which was to provide low-cost long-haul flights to a European hub airport; we would then link up with easyJet or Ryanair for onward connections within Europe. He liked it. Din shared my enthusiasm for airlines and travel and wanted to do something different.

We agreed that we wanted to be independent, apolitical, and that we wanted to create something totally new. Our style of working together was pretty clear too: I would be the front man, doing the marketing and publicity, and he'd do what he called the 'boring stuff in the background'.

Din and I have a true partnership. We each focus on what we're good at and play to those strengths. As a result, not much gets past us. We also agreed there and then that this was something we would build up, and put everything into it to succeed – not just get into it to make a quick buck. I said, 'Let's build a real business with actual profits that we can plough back in to drive growth. So, in years to come, we can look back and see something good that we've created.'

He was on board with that. He wanted to split the business 50/50 but I insisted on the extra 1 per cent because it was my idea.

At that point, still influenced by my love of music, I came up with the name Tune Air for our new airline project and decided on orange as the brand colour (I cared less about borrowing Stelios's orange than I did about being accused of copying Richard Branson's iconic red! Although I was quickly told by many people – pilots, government ministers and friends – that I should change to red, which has always been my preferred brand colour.) The details of the operation could have fitted on a napkin at this stage and the really pressing question was the one facing most entrepreneurs every time they try to launch something new: how do you start a business if you know nothing about the industry?

The only answer I had was to do something I was very good at: talking to people. I called people in my address book. Pretty much everybody laughed at the idea of me running an airline. So I rang Epsom and asked to be put in touch with anyone connected to the airline business. As always, Epsom were helpful and offered three people: Sir Brian Walpole, who was one of BA's most well-known pilots and had been the Queen's Concorde pilot; Clive Beddoe, who was one of the founding shareholders of a low-cost carrier called WestJet based in Canada; and my old Holman House mate, Mark Western, who was now a lawyer involved in aircraft leasing. I called Mark and asked him whether he could introduce me to Stelios to talk to him about my idea. Mark thought that that was probably a waste of my and Stelios's time because Stelios was on a different mission, but he did suggest I speak to GECAS (GE Capital Aviation Services) – the aviation leasing arm of GE and one of the biggest in the industry, with a fleet of nearly 2,000 planes leased out to airlines in seventy-six countries.

Nonetheless, I did write to Stelios because I admired what he'd done. He replied with a nice email and a polite refusal to get involved. I guess the success of my efforts in the aeroplane industry have proved his decision wrong, but I learned something important from the exchange – he did at least reply. Now that I'm in Stelios's position and get thousands of notes, emails and messages on social media from within and outside the company, I make sure that I go through every single one. Some of the great projects and ideas that we've come up with and seen through to execution have come from people getting in touch with me by email. It's a key part of company culture: you have to create an environment where people aren't afraid to share their ideas. So many flying routes, for example, have been introduced to AirAsia because staff have come forward and suggested there's a need for them.

When you receive countless ideas and requests from people it's easier to say 'no', but you never know what opportunity may come up. If Stelios had invested in me he could ultimately have part-owned a major Asian airline. So I always take cold calls or emails seriously; I investigate every single one of them. Some ideas might be preposterous but others can contain the germ of something special.

*

Our first attempts at sketching a business plan were chaotic, to put it mildly. We kicked off with a frenzied period trying to learn as much about the industry as we could, desperately trying to work out how much money we needed and how big a team could get our idea off the ground.

I based myself in the familiar surroundings of my old Warner office in Kuala Lumpur. I started to meet and talk to people to fill in the blank spaces in my understanding of what running an airline actually involved. In the first few months, Din and I hired a CFO, Rozman Bin Omar, and an accountant, Shireen Chia, and tasked them with working on the financial model. Din and I were the two main shareholders but even with my pay-off from Warner I was nowhere near as financially viable as I should have been. I roped in an old music industry contact, Aziz Bakar, as the third shareholder.

The office in Kuala Lumpur, a room that would be spacious for a single senior executive, was starting to feel a little cramped. I bought self-assembly desks when new people arrived and we ended up with a room stuffed with an odd selection of desks and chairs. It was chaos, and we took to calling it the War Room – many schemes were hatched there in our stealth operation to conquer the international airline industry.

We threw ourselves into the idea, going out to meet companies like Petronas, Malaysia's main oil and gas company, to negotiate fuel prices for planes and routes we didn't have. Mostly people laughed at us and said, 'Come back when you actually have a plane.' But we persisted, working round the clock, researching, calculating costs for parts and services that we didn't yet need; trying to understand the airline business and all the while adapting our model.

On Mark Western's recommendation I had connected with John Higgins at GECAS. Hoping that he'd be able to offer some advice, I sat down with John and outlined the plan which I'd developed so far: I wanted to lease Boeing 767s to fly to London from Kuala Lumpur. I think he thought I was a failed rock star with far too much money on my hands, but he was good enough to listen and make two important introductions. That meeting was the start of a relationship that has been crucial to AirAsia's success and one of the most satisfying business partnerships I've ever had.

The first introduction was to a man called Conor McCarthy. With over twenty years' experience in the airline business, he'd recently quit as Director of Group Operations at Ryanair to set up his own aviation consultancy. The second introduction was to Mike Jones, who was GECAS's representative in South East Asia. We clicked as soon as we met; Mike has been with us since that first introduction and remains a trusted advisor, colleague and business partner. He gave us a big break when we started out and has been the one with whom we've done pretty much all of our deals.

It was shortly after my meeting with John Higgins that I rang Conor McCarthy and was greeted by a thick Dublin accent.

'Hi, Conor, it's Tony Fernandes. I think John Higgins might have mentioned me to you?'

'Ah, sure, Tony. You're looking to start a low-cost

airline? You're probably only the fifth person who's had the idea in the last six months!'

'I think I can make it work. I'm just putting together a business plan. Can you come out to KL to help?'

'Sorry, mate, I can't come all that way. Tell you what, if you're serious, meet me at Stansted Airport and we can have a chat.'

Five days later, there I was standing at the Hertz Rent-A-Car desk. Sometimes people think that the origins of huge businesses can only take place in posh hotels or luxury resorts, but that's really not the case.

My phone rang. It was Conor.

'I can't see you. Where are you?'

He didn't know much about the world – he'd probably never been west of Galway or east of London – and from my name and my accent he probably had the idea that I was some six-foot, suave Antonio Banderas figure because he clearly didn't think I was me when he first saw me.

'I'm the short, fat Indian guy standing right in front of you.'

That broke the ice.

We sat down for coffee and I presented him with the business plan that we had so painstakingly drawn up. It was a pretty professional-looking document, neatly ring-bound, with tabs and indexes. We had put a lot of effort into it. But the thing about Conor is that he doesn't pull his punches – he describes himself as coming from the Ryanair School of Diplomacy. After about twenty seconds, I saw why.

'It looks great but the concept is crazy. Do you think you'll persuade Michael O'Leary [the owner of Ryanair]

and/or Stelios to agree to supply and take passengers flying to and from Malaysia from their networks in Europe?
That they'd agree to feed you passengers and allow your
passengers to access their routes? Why would they do
that?'

'They'd make more,' I argued.

'No, they wouldn't.'

I needed to understand why he was so definitive.

'Why wouldn't they?'

'Well, they already fill most of their planes – their load
factors are very high – and this would complicate their
business model. They would have to work out a whole new
business concept in terms of transferring baggage, the
accounting model in terms of who gets the money, in terms
of passengers who are delayed or who miss their flights,
who puts them up in a hotel, and so on. All of that compli-
cation you're pitching to a couple of guys whose automatic
reaction will be, *I don't need this, I've got 90 per cent load factors
and the business is doing fine.* Secondly, why would they talk to
you? You've got no experience in the business. They'd just
as soon turn round and say, *If I'm going to do it, I'll do it myself,
not with you.*'

I was reeling but saw that he was right and our plan was
hopeless.

Conor is a positive guy, though. He looks for solutions
not problems. He went on.

'Tell me, how many people live in Malaysia?'

'About 27 million.'

'OK, so what are you worrying about? Just go set up a
low-cost carrier in Malaysia that looks just like the models
in Europe; stop trying to invent something new. These

guys have made a load of money doing things simply. Sell your tickets over the web; don't use travel agents; get a single-class operation; put as many seats in the aircraft as you can; use the same type of aircraft; fly the planes morning until night and have the engineers work on them overnight. Be pure low cost.'

It was like the scales fell away from my eyes. Of course, all the airlines in South East Asia were charging an arm and a leg for travel and, as a consequence, very few people flew. A low-cost airline would democratize and revolutionize aviation in the region. In my dramatic way – and because after just two sips of coffee I trusted him – I took my carefully constructed business plan and ripped it in half in front of him.

'Let's start again.'

Even so, that early dream of fulfilling my promise to my mum to make it cheap to fly to London wasn't easily dismissed. I said to Conor the idea of low-cost long-haul would remain in the bottom drawer. I promised that one day I would properly explore it – which eventually I did, with the launch of AirAsia X.

Conor's experience at Ryanair was invaluable and I decided that we needed him on board as quickly as possible. Din and I reworked the business plan and I incorporated as much as I could from my meeting with Conor. We sent it off to him after a week, inviting him to come and help us.

I offered to pay him half in shares and half in cash, as we had no money. But he said no, he'd take it all in cash. Perhaps he didn't believe in the enterprise as much as Din and me.

Conor came out to Malaysia, and we carefully started to

reconstruct the business plan. With him on board, things started to come together over spring and early summer 2001. We were building a financial platform, identifying areas we needed to research and find experts in, and we built connections with GECAS to supply us with leased planes. It started to look like we might have the basics needed to launch an airline.

One morning, Aziz, Din and I were on our way to a meeting at the Ministry of Domestic Trade and Consumer Affairs in Dayabumi, Kuala Lumpur. I was reviewing our progress and feeling pretty optimistic before I suddenly had one of those thoughts that makes your stomach turn.

'We don't know how to get an airline licence,' I said.

We looked at each other and slumped back in our chairs, before Aziz said some words that are common in Malaysian business.

'We need political connections. And we have none.'

Then I had a brainwave. We were about to meet Dato' Pahamin Ab Rajab. He was the secretary-general of the ministry; we'd worked together to take on the music pirates when I was first at Warner in Malaysia. Before that he'd been in the Ministry of Transport. He was one scary guy – a man of fierce, passionate temper but honest and straight. Exactly the kind of person I like, in other words.

So I said, 'Why don't we ask Pahamin to be our chairman?'

He was the only person we knew and, as it happened, probably a good fit. The others thought I was mad – not for the first time – but we had nothing to lose.

As soon as we raised the idea, Pahamin agreed without hesitation, only asking us what we needed. He was one of the few that didn't laugh in our faces. We said the most pressing problem he could help with was to get us in to see Prime Minister Mahathir bin Mohamad. We knew this was a big ask, as the two didn't exactly see eye to eye; they had very different views on how to implement democracy and how civil servants should work. But Pahamin agreed to try.

True to his word, Pahamin somehow got us an appointment with the Prime Minister in July 2001. It was our only shot at getting this low-cost, short-haul airline off the ground.

The meeting was set for 11.00 a.m. at the Prime Minister's office in the government district of Putrajaya – about twenty-five miles outside Kuala Lumpur. The building, Perdana Putra, is one of the most imposing buildings in Malaysia – a huge six-storey complex which has two wings attached to an impressive central structure, topped off by an onion-shaped glazed mosaic main dome, a replica of Masjid Zahir in Alor Setar, Kedah. The main dome is surrounded by four smaller domes. It's a place built to make you feel small.

I turned up at 6.00 a.m. having not slept a wink. The main gates were still locked, so I simply sat down on the steps and waited. There was so much riding on this meeting, and the fact that the Prime Minister wasn't a big fan of Pahamin played on my mind. The PM had been in office since 1981; he knew everyone and everything. If he agreed to grant us an airline licence, my – our – dream could move a big step forward; if he refused, it was dead in the water. I was terrified. Conor had already flown back to Ireland as his work was pretty much done, while Din had gone to

Australia, so it was just me, Aziz, Pahamin and our financial controller, Cheah.

I finally got into the building at about 8.30 after some official or other had taken pity on me. I think the official might have recognized me from my Warner days because he asked, 'Why are you here? Have you come to speak to him about music piracy?'

'No', I replied. 'I want to start an airline.'

He laughed at me but I was more than used to it by then. Aziz turned up, and the official continued, 'But it's a bad day to see him. He's going to be in a bad mood. He's seeing the leader of the opposition first thing.'

My heart sank a little further – it wasn't like we could reschedule but the odds were stacking up against us. I remained optimistic as I knew we had a good plan to present.

Pahamin had arrived and we could see he was talking to some pretty serious-looking people in black suits. Aziz and I walked over to them. Pahamin's face didn't radiate happiness.

'You won't believe it. The next people in to see the PM after the opposition are Malaysia Airlines. They're going to be talking about their MYR [Malaysian ringgit] eight billion restructuring. I don't think he'll be very interested in granting a licence to a new airline if the national carrier is failing so badly.'

My heart sank further still. I was wondering if I should start applying to PricewaterhouseCoopers for an accounting job. The chances of the PM granting a low-cost airline licence to a group of aviation outsiders were slim if he was in a happy mood; if he was already carrying bad feelings from the two previous meetings, we were toast.

Our turn for an audience finally arrived. The walk to his office door seemed to take for ever; and, once we were inside, I felt like a five-year-old in the headmaster's study. Overwhelmed by the size and power of the office and the man, I was terrified.

'Make it fast, I'm sick,' he snapped.

So, a meeting with the opposition, Malaysia Airlines and now, third problem, he was sick. Again, thoughts of PricewaterhouseCoopers sprang into my mind.

I'm a great believer in the idea that nothing is ever wasted. Before the meeting, I'd bought a copy of my final album at Warner – the live concert featuring the PM's own pet project, the Malaysian Philharmonic Orchestra.

'Before we start, Prime Minister,' I said, barely able to keep the tremble out of my voice, 'can I give you this? It was the last album I made at Warner.'

The mood softened, but I still had to give the presentation. It was met with silence. The only reaction I got from him was the occasional scowl and a wry smile when I said I was going to take on and destroy Singapore Airlines (SIA). When I finished my presentation, the room was once again silent. Finally the Prime Minister spoke: 'I like this model. I like you guys. I think you're going to succeed. And you're going to succeed because you have passion and you're not from the airline business.'

It helped that the Prime Minister knew his stuff when it came to airlines. Having visited Ryanair to see how they'd compete with the more established Aer Lingus, he told us that he'd advised Malaysia Airlines to create a low-cost airline – which they had never done.

'If you're good I'll give you all of Malaysia Airlines'

domestic routes. You have my blessing.' For half a second, I felt on top of the world. Ecstatic and relieved.

'But,' the Prime Minister uttered and my heart sank yet again, 'you've got to buy an airline. I won't give you a licence to create a new one because I've had too many failed airlines.'

We were back to square one and came out of the meeting with a black cloud over our heads. How were we going to find and buy an existing airline? Forever the optimist, I said: 'Well, we've got to try and find one.' We had come too far to give it all up now.

Over the next few days we shopped around for airlines to buy. Aziz and I approached an airline called Pelangi Air but when we went to see them they said, 'Give us $40 million and we'll turn the airline round for you.'

We looked at the books and it was a joke – only God could have turned that company round.

We politely declined.

A few weeks later, and no further forward, I went to play golf. While I was on the green, I saw the corporate communications director of DRB-HICOM – one of Malaysia's leading manufacturers. I knew they owned a tiny airline called AirAsia but, to be completely honest, I didn't really know what it was, where it flew to or anything concrete about it at all. It was so insignificant that, even as desperate as we were, it hadn't appeared on our list of potential airlines to buy. Still, I went up to him and said, 'Hey, I hear you have an airline.'

'Yeah,' he scoffed. 'Wanna buy it?'

'Yes,' I said confidently.

'You can have it tomorrow,' he replied. 'We don't need it.'

I went home that night and frantically tried to learn more about AirAsia. Din and I made enquiries and found out that it had a few domestic routes, two 737-300s and about 200 staff. It had been set up in the mid nineties by Tan Sri Yahaya Ahmad, the founder of DRB-HICOM, with the aim of becoming the second largest carrier, after MAS (Malaysian Airline System), in Malaysia. Tragically, he died in 1997 and with him went the dream of creating an airline. AirAsia had been nothing but a burden on DRB's books ever since. So by 2001 it had amassed MYR 40 million debt and was going nowhere.

For Din and me it was a lifeline. We went to see the deputy CEO of DRB the next day and he was happy to do a deal, to say the least.

'You can have the airline tomorrow. How much do you want to pay for it?'

'One ringgit?' I asked, tongue in cheek, as that was the equivalent of about fifty US cents.

'You can have the airline for one ringgit provided you remove our corporate guarantee from GECAS,' the deputy CEO offered.

I immediately thought, 'Damn,' as I should have got them to pay *me* for it.

So AirAsia – a tiny, unknown and unloved airline – was ours for the taking *if* we could persuade GECAS to release DRB-HICOM from an important financial constraint.

A corporate guarantee is an instrument that is provided by a parent company when one of its smaller subsidiaries enters into a long-term agreement with a third party. In this case, DRB-HICOM guaranteed payment of the leases for the aircraft for as long as the lease was in place.

So, we needed to get GECAS's approval for the acquisition because they needed the guarantee that the leases for the two planes that AirAsia operated would be paid. Of course, DRB-HICOM wanted to sell the company but didn't want to continue to provide the guarantee – they wanted to walk clean away from the airline.

It wasn't a done deal. GECAS had entered into the leases for the planes because DRB-HICOM owned the airline. Why would they be sympathetic to our plan? We had no experience in the airline industry and no money. On paper, it wasn't a great offer.

I was put in touch with Mike Jones at GECAS to whom I said, 'Look, I studied Portfolio Risk Management at university, if you treat me as every other credit applicant, then of course I'm not going to qualify and you'll turn me down. Fair enough. But if I make this airline work, I'm going to be a massive customer. I might be leasing or buying 1,000 engines from you. Go on, take a risk, it's two planes out of your 2,000. AirAsia isn't growing now – you'll get the money for the remainder of the contract but you won't make any more money. Go on, take a leap of faith, give up the guarantee.'

I'm not sure he entirely believed that I could turn Air-Asia round but perhaps he saw the same passion in me as the Prime Minister had.

He gave me approval to go to GE Capital in Fairchild, Connecticut, to make the same presentation to the main board, warning me that I should not turn up in my normal scruffy outfit. I bought myself a serious suit and prepared thoroughly for the meeting. When I walked into the boardroom I saw that everyone else was in jeans, of course.

I did the presentation again, tackled the same objections, made the same points as I had to Mike. As a sweetener, we agreed that we'd give them first refusal on providing the next five planes we'd lease so it would be an ongoing relationship. Eventually they agreed.

The corporate guarantee was removed; we could go ahead and buy AirAsia for MYR 1.

However, every time it looked like we were headed into calmer waters, another wave of problems hit us. On 8 September 2001, the night before we were due to sign, we were suddenly told there was one other AirAsia shareholder, a company called Mofaz. And they refused to sell – they were being cute by appealing to the Prime Minister to stop us. The decision was due the following morning and it was on a knife edge. Once again our futures seemed to be in the PM's hands.

I couldn't sleep that night. We had an airline within our grasp but it was quite possible that we could lose it. After an agonizing wait, the PM denied Mofaz's request and we were allowed to proceed. I don't know why and I don't care to dwell on it, but the stress of those few months was unbelievable. We signed on 9 September 2001, subject to due diligence.

The due diligence was necessary because Din and I were applying for mortgages on our houses to get some cash – it really was all or nothing. DRB-HICOM could have held out for the due diligence to be approved but they allowed us to run the airline for three months while they paid the costs and the due diligence was completed.

At the last minute they said they wanted to keep a 10 per cent stake in the business, but Din was smart and refused.

I had been quite happy to give it to them but he realized that it meant we wouldn't be fully autonomous. That's why we work so well together – he sees things that I don't (and vice versa).

AirAsia had MYR 40 million ($20 million) debt when we took it on and was, I was told, losing around MYR 4 million a month. As part of the deal, DRB-HICOM took on half of that and we shouldered the other half. The three main debtors were MAS, Petronas and Malaysian Airports; I went to each of them and promised that we'd pay up on time. It was a point of principle to make sure our suppliers trusted and respected us. It paid dividends because we reduced the interest rate on the debts as a result.

Now we had an airline and three months' grace to start to turn things around. It was an amazing feeling after months of stress. We had worked unbelievably hard figuring out how a whole industry functioned, modelling a new way of operating a business and overcoming what seemed like – and still seems like – impossible odds. We drew a short breath before throwing ourselves back into the action.

Only two days after we signed the contract, I was watching the Malaysian football team lose to Laos when my phone started pinging with texts. The messages carried news that I simply couldn't believe. I drove home and turned on *Bloomberg News* just as the Twin Towers collapsed. Time stood still. It was surreal. I sat there trying to process all the thoughts and emotions this barbaric act had stirred in me. I watched people jumping out of windows, an image previously unthinkable and one not easily forgotten. My heart broke for all the people involved in the tragedy: those suffering inside the tower and the families whose lives would now be shattered.

My thoughts also turned to the aviation industry and whether our brand-new airline was going to survive the troubles ahead. Traumatized as I and the whole world were, we had the opportunity to start something new, and I strongly believed that people would still want to fly. It's incredibly difficult to carry on in the face of such tragedy but I never doubted for a second that we would.

After the initial shock of 9/11 subsided, Din rang me and asked: 'Shall we still do this?'

'Yeah, we've got so far,' I answered. 'Someone must be on our side; it looks really, really bad but people still have to fly to Penang. Let's do it. Almost even more so now, we've got to make sure people can fly.'

We had set out with a dream of giving everyone the chance to fly, and that's what we still had to do. I felt that I owed it to the people who worked at AirAsia and to our future passengers to show up to work as usual. The model we had been implementing would enrich people's lives. I had to focus on that.

The short-term economics were horrible in every conceivable way: the price of oil was going through the roof and passenger confidence was shaken. In every sense, starting an airline at this moment in history seemed like the most foolish business idea ever. But I knew we had to do it.

So we went ahead.

Four days after 9/11, we got our first piece of good news. GECAS approached us with a proposal.

We had been going to swap AirAsia's existing two

737-300s for 737-200s because the 300s were too expensive for us to run. The 200s were smaller and older, and our pilots were freaking out in anticipation, because some of the controls were still hydraulic dials rather than digital.

Ray from GECAS said, 'Look, lease rates have collapsed because of 9/11. I'll cut you a deal. Keep the 737-300s and we'll halve the rate.'

That changed the numbers for us dramatically: our revenues went up because the 300s carried about twenty extra seats, and the costs were reduced because they were more efficient and powerful, meaning that fuel costs and flight times were reduced. Conor McCarthy and I messaged each other, concluding that 'there really is a God'. Ryanair had started with 200s so I had assumed that we were fine following their lead, but keeping the 300s was a game-changer. GECAS and AirAsia have worked brilliantly together ever since.

We had aeroplanes (registrations 9M-AAA and 9M-AAB), we had a licence, we had staff and we had even inherited some routes. This was all very well, but we still needed money to run the airline. Between the four of us we simply didn't have the cash. Din and I were trying to remortgage our houses to have something to put in. We'd forecast that we'd need MYR 20 million to get the business running, so while I had been off negotiating with GECAS, Din had secured the money through a financier. I hadn't met him but he believed in the idea and had committed to the money. He would, once the deal was signed, be our partner, owning 50 per cent of the company. Not ideal but we had no other option. I went off to his office in

Kuala Lumpur to meet him and present what we had done, who we'd hired, the business plan, and to brief him on the initial discussions with GECAS about the planes.

About halfway through the conversation, he raised his hand to stop me. He asked me, 'Why have you done all this without letting me know? I'm your partner.'

I reacted in my normal candid way: 'Well, you haven't signed anything yet, or given us any money, so you're not a partner yet.'

I didn't mean to upset him or piss him off. It was absolutely true. But I could have been a little less direct, I suppose, because he didn't react well at all. It was my first experience of successful, wealthy businessmen and the way they expect to be treated. Sometimes their ego gets the better of them and they don't like it when you challenge or upset the way they expect things to be done.

He thought I was being flippant; whereas in my mind, I was just stating a fact – I'm a black and white person, which can get me into trouble. As I've grown older I've grown a bit wiser but I've upset a lot of people along the way. In fact, recently a friend texted me an observation about my relationships in business: 'You can educate but also provoke: you have a talent for that . . .'

My openness and directness had led me into trouble again. But as a leader I think it's much better than hedging and making people second-guess. You need to lead through clarity, not manipulation.

When I left that meeting, I called Din and said, 'I think I may have messed up the 20 million.'

So we were back to having no money to run the airline. When he heard about it, to his eternal credit, Pahamin didn't lay into me or rant and rave, he just said, 'Tony, given the way you like to do things, it might be for the best. I can't imagine you and Din running every decision past someone else. It just won't work.'

Din and I agreed that we'd just have to run it on the cash we took in. If we wanted to operate a low-cost airline we'd have to practise what we preached and strip away every frill. We'd need to survive hand to mouth.

Like I said, nothing was easy.

After signing the deal we met with some of the existing AirAsia staff at DRB-HICOM's offices. I was nervous – I was used to doing presentations, but about artists and bands, not about aeroplanes and passengers. Yet it was also an electrifying feeling because I'd never thought I had the balls to be an entrepreneur. I'd run a music company but all of a sudden I owned an airline – an airline with just two planes, but an airline nonetheless.

I walked into a large office in DRB-HICOM's head-quarters in Kuala Lumpur. Lined up, hugging the walls and windows, were thirty to forty of the existing AirAsia staff. There were engineers, cabin crew, pilots and ground handlers, all looking at me sceptically. All they knew about me was that I was some music industry guy who had a wild idea about offering cheap air travel in Malaysia.

I outlined the model to the staff, who listened in silence. I'm not sure whether it was out of respect or disbelief. After I'd finished, the chief engineer put his hand up. 'Malaysians want and expect service. Can no frills work in Malaysia?'

'Look, if you set the fare low enough, I think it will. And we can still offer service. We're not going to be like

Ryanair, because it doesn't cost anything to smile. We'll have rules and regulations that passengers need to follow but we'll be nice. I'm not appealing to the people travelling on MAS or Singapore Airlines now – I'm trying to create a new market for people who've never flown before.'

There was another moment of silence before one of the cabin crew piped up: 'This is brilliant. I believe we'll be bigger than MAS one day. Just listening to the energy and passion you bring to this is inspiring. We haven't heard that kind of attitude for six years. I'm feeling very proud now to be part of this.'

At that moment, it had all been worth it.

6. Flying High

Soundtrack: 'Tubthumping (I Get Knocked Down)' by Chumbawamba

You never know what's going to be thrown at you when you start a business. And it may have been a completely ridiculous idea to start an airline with no experience, particularly in the dark shadow of 9/11. But when I look back to the early years of AirAsia I'm struck by just how many unpredictable, huge problems we faced and survived. I'm convinced that our young company grew stronger after each crisis and we are where we are now because of each of them.

Though my first staff meeting had been met with a positive response, the next staff session we had was a little trickier. The routes AirAsia were flying when we took over were twice a day to Kota Kinabalu and twice a day to Kuching. That's all the airline covered, despite holding landing rights to other locations. Our business model required the ground crew and pilots to double the aircraft utilization from six to twelve hours a day; and to reduce the turnaround (the length of time between arrival at the gate and departure) to twenty-five minutes. I thought it was going to be a tough sell but as I walked into the room all the pilots and engineers stood up and saluted. I was thrown and quite amused. They were not aware of my style of management, that was for sure.

'Sit down. Chill,' I said in my music industry style. If I

had never been saluted before, then I certainly don't think they'd ever been told to 'chill'.

As I outlined the proposals, I sensed some pushback from the pilots and the engineers. There were concerns about cooling the plane's brakes enough in the time, as well as more obvious worries about doubling the amount of flying the pilots would be doing. I privately thanked GECAS again for letting us retain the better 737-300s; if we'd suggested this while operating 200s instead I don't think there would have been many people left in the room.

The consensus amongst the staff, though, was that they'd give it a go. As we left the room, we met a few of the DRB-HICOM directors, who asked how it had gone. Aziz, always one with a quick tongue, just smiled and said: 'Great. They can't wait to be out from under you lot.'

It was true for the staff but I have to say that DRB-HICOM couldn't have been more accommodating or helpful to us.

We finally signed for and took over the airline on 8 December 2001, once the due diligence had been completed. The pens and documents were being put away when DRB's chief executive looked at me and raised an eyebrow. I thought this was odd but smiled. Then he held out his right hand, palm up, and said, 'Come on then, pay up.'

'What?'

'You and Din owe us one ringgit.'

I laughed and took my wallet out. No cash. I looked at Din. He pulled his wallet out of his back pocket, looked inside and shrugged.

'Can you lend us the money? We seem not to have any cash.'

When the laughing subsided, the CEO found a note which he gave to us and we ceremoniously handed it back. The purchase of AirAsia was complete. I don't think Din or I ever paid the money back . . . so technically we didn't pay anything for our airline.

From that moment on, running AirAsia became the most exciting and exhausting rollercoaster I've ever been on; we really were flying by the seats of our pants. Our staff knew how to do their jobs well but we, as management, had to knit the whole process together and it was clear that it was going to take a bit of time.

Fortunately, we made some key decisions that helped bring everyone together. When we took over the full operation in December, DRB-HICOM let us know that a bonus was due to the staff. The bill came in at MYR 1 million, which would have wiped out all of our cash and forced us to look for outside investment again. DRB were supportive once more and they agreed to pay half. Even so, we had less of a cushion than we felt comfortable with. Captain Chin, to date our longest-serving employee and a company legend, says that paying that bonus brought any remaining sceptical staff onside. It would have been easier to defer or not to pay at all that period, but Din and I felt strongly that we had to treat the team fairly. The mantra, 'Your business is your people,' is still one of the strongest elements of the AirAsia culture.

When our first flight took off, my heart really did swell with pride. Not even a year before, I'd seen Stelios talk on a television set in an old pub on Hampstead Heath; now I was watching my own plane lift off into the skies.

However, there was so much still to do to convert this

tiny airline into a low-cost giant, it seemed we barely had time to celebrate or even mark the first flight before getting back to work. We couldn't implement our low-cost model immediately. We relied on existing routes and structures for the first few weeks until we could convert the planes and introduce the full low-cost plan. This was based on increasing the number of seats in the cabin from 124 to 148 by ripping out business class completely. Every extra seat we sold would make a difference, so on the day we took over operations I ceremoniously padlocked the business class lounge at Subang Airport, and then over the course of six months we converted the planes.

Our fares were aggressively low. The normal fare to Kota Kinabalu was MYR 400, but we were offering seats at MYR 149.99.

However, we made the tickets non-refundable. They were so cheap that we decided it was up to the passenger to turn up. At that time, passengers still claimed refunds if they couldn't fly but we made it clear that unless the passenger informed us within forty-eight hours of buying the ticket, we would not refund the purchase. If they did tell us within forty-eight hours, we agreed that we would try to do a credit swap and issue the ticket for another time – but the passenger would have to pay the difference if the new ticket was more expensive. The swap would also attract an admin fee.

After a few weeks, we were ready to make our first low-cost flight. I got the staff together for a meeting the night before.

We ran through all their questions and restated our aim about being no frills. If the staff had ideas for saving money, we said, we wanted to hear them. A stewardess raised her hand.

'In the model, you mention selling food on the plane . . .?'

'Yes.'

'So where's that going to come from?'

There was a collective intake of breath. I looked around me, picked up my jacket and told five people to follow me. We jumped in our cars and headed for the nearest Carrefour supermarket. We stocked up with sandwiches, drinks and water and paid for it on my credit card. We brought it back, loaded it on to the planes and were ready to go.

'How much are we selling it for?'

'Just don't make a loss on it – otherwise I don't mind.'

Like I say, flying by the seat of our pants. We learned and adapted fast: we borrowed, loaned or bartered for just about everything. We didn't steal, although we came very close when one of the pilots pointed out that there was too much wear on one of the plane's tyres. Our engineer suggested we 'borrow' a tyre from a competing airline and replace it once ours was repaired. We dragged in a third party to arbitrate and fortunately they passed the tyre for use.

Peter Talalla, an experienced fleet manager, had joined us when we were still in the set-up phase of AirAsia. He had been an airline pilot and I'd been put in touch with him through my growing network of airline contacts. As we were compiling the business plan, we'd realized that we lacked any pilot input. We were committed to changing the number of seats but had no idea how much extra fuel we'd consequently need. Peter came along to talk to me and I realized that he was going to be a big help – he'd been fleet manager at MAS as well as being an experienced pilot.

Peter turned his hand to everything – exactly the kind of person I like to have around. I'd ask him about baggage handling or turnaround times or fuel and he'd get on the case. When we started operating, he used his contacts to fill in the missing pieces of the jigsaw; in particular, he found a ground handler who wanted to work with us and saved us the expense of investing in that equipment; Din's brother helped us out with insurance; Select Aviation helped us with cabin crew training and then Singapore Technologies helped out with the maintenance. If we could get anything on loan or hire purchase we did, because we had to conserve as much cash as possible.

Other incidental revenue streams helped us. We inherited from the old AirAsia a contract to provide travel for the hajj pilgrimage and also some military charter flights.

The hajj was a big logistical headache. We flew from 18–20,000 passengers in the space of about twenty days in February 2002, allowing for all of the worshippers to complete the five-day pilgrimage. The complexity of that kind of contract (which we'd got from DRB-HICOM) was all-consuming for a small, inexperienced team. Peter Talalla led the project, working through problems using whatever written resources he could lay his hands on, talking to anyone who might have useful tips and liaising with the Tabung Haji (National Haji Fund) to make sure that all the requirements were met. It was extraordinarily complex but worth it because it generated MYR 20 million and we made a clear profit of about MYR 6 million. That inflow of cash kept us going for another few months.

*

The dash to Carrefour had highlighted how much we didn't know, so I decided the best way forward was to learn everything from the ground up. From day one it felt like I lived at the offices in Subang and I started a routine that I still practise today: I worked all the jobs in the airline. You can't be an effective CEO unless you're prepared to get your hands dirty. I think many leaders don't actually know what's going on; they get their information second- or third-hand and then they make the wrong decision. I decided I was going to learn everything. So I went in the simulator, to learn how to fly a plane; I learned how to change wheels and knew everything about the engine; I was cabin crew and I checked passengers in – which is the hardest job – and I carried bags. I've learned so much as a result and it makes a critical difference to the atmosphere of the company.

Learning on the job with the staff means I can listen to problems and make a call with some authority. I can also become part of the staff's narrative about their jobs. Being a ramp boy means you're carrying two tons of bags off a flight and then two tons back on to the plane, which is physically challenging to say the least.

The first time I had a go at being cabin crew, it reminded me of my time at the Cavendish. When you see cabin staff you don't realize that they've probably had to get up at 4.00 or 5.00 a.m.; that their working day will consist of five or six flights, serving food and drinks, then cleaning the plane and handling the boarding within a twenty-five-minute turnaround. All the while they have to smile, be positive, deal with multiple questions and a range of complaints, and be the public face of the airline. It's not an easy job and they work extremely hard. I was smiling as I pushed the trolley down the aisle, serving food and doing pretty well, I thought. A man asked for a can of Coke. I nodded, smiled and picked out the can quickly, but as I lifted the ring pull, my AirAsia colleague on the other side of the trolley put her hand out to stop me.

'Don't open it!' she said.

I looked at her as if she was slightly mad, ignored her instruction, handed over the can and, proud of my knowledge of the prices, said, 'That's three ringgit, please.'

The man looked at me in horror and handed the can back. He had assumed the drinks were free.

It's a small illustration of the kind of things you learn. Customer interactions are never easy. In fact, I'd say dealing with customers is the hardest job in the airline business; but dealing with customers who are travelling low cost is doubly difficult because they push as hard as they can for more. When we say 'no frills', we mean 'no frills'. You'll get fantastic service for free but we charge for everything else because our fares are so low.

AirAsia is one of the largest companies, and certainly one of the largest airlines, that has no union. And that's not because of the law: Malaysia Airlines has forty unions. It's because AirAsia staff don't see the point of outside representation when we have such strong internal dialogue. Part of that is through internal networks, but also because I get out there and do the jobs on the ground.

A few years into our business, when we upgraded the fleet to Airbus, there was an issue for the baggage handlers. They were used to throwing bags into the hold on the 737s but the Airbus hold is a few inches higher. The handlers came to me saying that they needed belt-loaders because the physical strain was getting too much. I refused because it was a cost we couldn't afford at the time. Not long after, I was doing my turn with the baggage guys again and I was allocated an Indonesian route. Now people who fly with us generally bring their houses with them but people who fly to Indonesia seem to bring their neighbour's house too! I ended up throwing hundreds of bags into the hold and my back was breaking. At the end of the day, I turned to the baggage handlers I'd been working with and said, 'All right guys. You're on. You're right, I'm wrong. We'll go sort it out tomorrow.'

The next day I put in an order for belt-loaders.

If I hadn't done that, if I hadn't gone down and actually done the job, I'd have destroyed many people's backs, created a needless attitude of resentment and probably brought in a union as a result. Recently a pilot told me that our pilots were approached many times by MAS pilots suggesting they join their union; but, the pilot said, they replied, 'Why? If we need to talk to Tony we just call him up – we work things out directly. It's much better.'

Getting out and doing all the different jobs or walking around head office are essential parts of my working life. As a CEO I don't think there is any other way of getting to know your staff, getting to understand their jobs, frustrations and fears and gaining their respect. To this day, I know more about every aspect of the company than anyone else because I've done all the jobs. No reports, spreadsheets or interviews can replace that hands-on knowledge. I encourage all my management or office-based staff to fly as much as possible because you have to keep in touch with the customers and the front-line staff.

This also works to keep communication open and unrestricted. In the last year or so, one cabin crew had been caught stealing. She'd been dealt with by the right people but she still felt able to text me directly to say that she was sorry and to ask for a second chance. Having access like that is worth seven HR departments in my view.

At our management conference in 2017 in Phuket, Thailand, I had a go at our head office staff for hiding behind their laptops or in meeting rooms. As a company grows, it's critical that everyone gets out and talks to everyone else and keeps a realistic handle on the day-to-day business. The moment you schedule wall-to-wall meetings all day every day is the moment that you start to lose your grasp on what you're supposed to be doing. In our case, running a world-beating low-cost airline. Losing sight of that is how a great corporate culture can start to wither and die.

The two biggest causes of unhappiness in an organization are offices and job titles. For years I have wanted to remove job titles from business cards – apart from emphasizing the title rather than the role, they shut down a conversation about what you do at a company. Far better to explain than be defined by your title.

Offices are a nightmare. One of the earliest things I did in the first AirAsia offices was to hire some contractors to knock down all the office partitions. If there is no haggling for this or that office or space, everyone can just focus on doing their job and not stress about so-and-so who has an office or has a bigger office, and so on. The new HQ (called RedQ) at Kuala Lumpur International

Airport (KLIA), which we designed together, has no offices. Everything is open plan apart from a series of glass-walled meeting rooms. It's so important to have a space without brick walls: it encourages people to speak freely and it eliminates office envy.

The other important decision I took was to try to bring everyone together. The staff were originally quite segregated: pilots spoke to pilots, engineers to engineers, cabin crew to cabin crew. I thought it was detrimental to the business because each group could help the other. So we also had lots of parties – all of them with no budget! – but it really did help people bond.

With no money to take on MAS and Singapore Airlines, I felt the strongest weapons we had were our culture and the fact that we were small and agile. We had no preconceptions about a 'right' way of doing things. We could disrupt as much as we liked because we didn't know any better.

The culture of integration and a diverse, multicultural staff goes right back to my childhood reading and my travel in the USA and Australia. When we set up AirAsia Thailand I found that the pilots wouldn't travel to the plane with the cabin crew despite repeated requests from management. So I took twelve Malaysian pilots and twelve Malaysian cabin crew off to Thailand and forced them to get the bus together to show the Thais how AirAsia works. Within two years there were two Malay–Thai marriages within AirAsia Thailand.

We always kept in mind that AirAsia versus MAS was the ultimate David and Goliath situation. MAS were owned by a combination of the government and the stock market so they were unimaginably rich in our eyes; they had 120 planes where we had just two and they had a virtual monopoly on most of the domestic routes – our target market. So the only thing we could do was to be better, which meant be more innovative, provide fantastic value for money and customer service, and react much faster to changing market conditions.

We were the new boys, and being new we had no influence. Our only option was to disrupt. This has become a bit of a cliché now but in 2001 it was still quite a novel idea. We didn't try to match the competition, we tried to do things differently and, by doing that, changed the shape of the market. It's a common misconception that disruption is destructive; it isn't, it's creative. In this approach I was influenced by a book called *Blue Ocean Strategy*. We came into the Malaysian airline market and we didn't set about stealing routes from the existing players; instead we looked for new routes, we *created* new areas of the market where we were the first stallholders. The others would have to play catch-up. Disruption isn't about destroying the competition, it's about changing the market to your advantage.

We'd made it to February 2002, and were improving the airline, surviving on the cash we generated and even starting to chip away at some of the debt. Then one of the planes (9M-AAB) got hit by a bird strike and was grounded while the engine was fixed. The plane was on a night flight to Kuching when it happened, captained by one of my most experienced pilots, Adrian Jenkins (now group director of Flight Operations). He called me as soon as the engineer had given his report. When I heard, I couldn't believe it. I'd never even heard that this was potentially a problem – how stupid must birds be to fly into an aircraft engine? Then the consequences became apparent: the aircraft would be out of action for eleven days while the engine was repaired. Effectively that meant that our fleet was halved for the entire period. Imagine if that happened to British Airways or Ryanair. Our scale was tiny but the relative economic effect was the same.

My reaction, I've been told, made a big difference to the morale of the company. For a start, I didn't freak out. The first thing I did was check that all the passengers and the crew were OK. The staff really responded to that because I didn't scream or shout or panic and didn't blame anyone, but demonstrated that safety was the number-one priority. And then I gathered everyone. 'We were aiming to do twenty-five-minute turnarounds, now we're going to make them twenty minutes,' I told them. 9M-AAA flew twenty-four hours for eleven days – we never cancelled a flight. There were delays but we worked foot-to-the-floor to honour our passengers' tickets. By the time the engine was repaired, we had shown how committed we were to giving everyone the opportunity to fly.

Anyone who worked at AirAsia then knew the intensity of the experience and I genuinely believe the episode was the making of the company – not only in the eyes of our customers but of the staff as well. If you go through a test like that and come out the other side the experience forges an unbelievably strong culture and sense of belief. It also injects a huge amount of confidence into a young company. People began to believe the unbelievable: that maybe there was something about this ridiculous idea, that maybe we could really make things happen. On a purely practical level, it also demonstrated to the pilots and engineers that a twenty-five-minute turnaround was possible, even beatable.

No sooner had we lurched out of that crisis than we hit a different kind of problem, one that was potentially fatal to the business. After we'd fixed 9M-AAB, Chinese New Year holiday season at the end of February was on the horizon. A year before in Stansted, Conor and I had discussed selling tickets over the web, cutting out the travel agents who were making 7 per cent on every sale. At that point, though, we were using the sales system inherited from the old AirAsia and had not switched to our planned web-based direct-to-customer booking engine. (Ryanair used a system called 'Open Skies', which Conor had mentioned, but I wasn't ready to look at that yet; there were too many other headaches – like bird strikes – to deal with.) As we approached the holiday season, I was getting reports of huge sales – 65,000 seats for the end of February and we had only been going for a couple of months. We were looking at an 85 per cent load factor. I hoped the cash would enable us to invest and develop further.

I had been a bit concerned about the role of the travel agents, and not just for the commission they took. There was a sense that MAS had a firm grip on the whole agent network; they had more routes, more planes, more capacity and more clout. Although there was no evidence of this happening, I was genuinely worried that, if an agent started selling non-MAS tickets, MAS would stop dealing with that travel agent.

This was the background to the day before the holiday started, when my daily load report appeared showing we suddenly had an extra 25,000 seats. When I checked what had happened, I was as angry as I had been for a long, long time. It seemed the travel agents had put place-holders on the seats they'd 'bought', so that if someone walked in off the streets, they would have a seat to sell them straight away. They'd effectively taken all my 'inventory' and prevented me from selling it in case someone wanted it; once the opportunity to sell had passed, they returned the seats. I was stuck with 25,000 seats I had no way of selling and we were back in crisis mode.

I rang Conor straight away and said, 'Put me in touch with the guy who runs Navitaire [the company that owns the 'Open Skies' web booking system]. I'm going to Minneapolis tomorrow.' We signed a deal within a couple of days of me arriving and had the system installed within a month.

The travel agent experience also brought home to Din and me just how hard we had to focus on cost to make our model work. Our mantra 'Cost is king' came from this period because we looked at every single line of every contract, looked at every cost line and every revenue line to see if we could squeeze more money out of operations. So, for example, a company offered to install a TV panel on the headrest of each seat. The company who proposed the deal said they'd pay for the screens and installation and we'd split the advertising revenues. It looked like it would be all upside, but Din and I thought it through and rejected it for three reasons: the first was that the screens added more weight to the plane, which would increase our fuel costs; the second was that it added more complexity to the plane's wiring and added another possible cause of malfunction; lastly, we wanted the crew to sell products directly to the customers (if the passengers are watching a screen, they'll buy less). We were ruthless in cutting costs and ruthless in sticking to our model.

And that model itself was starting to make bigger waves. When we ran our first ad for a fare of MYR 9.99 to Kota Kinabalu, the country went bananas. The phone system physically melted – the demand caused the main switchboard to over-heat – so there was a stampede at the airport. Our staff were overwhelmed and our customers were shoving each other to get to the ticket counters. After that experience we invested in a numbered-ticket dispenser to organize the crowds.

Things were starting to move in our direction. We bought a third plane – an old Air Afrique 737 – which we had painted in our red livery before it was delivered. The other two AirAsia planes were still in the old AirAsia colours because we couldn't have them on the ground long enough to get them painted. So when 9M-AAC came in to land at Subang dressed up in our rebranded AirAsia red, it was a big moment. We all stood on the observation deck as the plane approached and it stirred memories of waiting for my mum to come back from her Tupperware trips. My heart skipped a beat as the plane landed. One cabin crew, Andrea Pinto, started crying. She turned to me and said, 'Five years we've waited for a third plane and in just three months since you took over, we have it!'

I'd underestimated just how much the staff wanted AirAsia to move on and how frustrated they were by the lack of progress under the previous management. Her pride and ambition stirred me.

Back in September, when we first signed the deal with DRB-HICOM, I had approached the government to ask if AirAsia could keep flying out of Subang Airport – it would have meant so much to me to be able to have my airline based at the airport where my love of flying had started. KLIA had recently been built and we were under huge pressure to relocate our operations there. We fought long and hard but the government wouldn't give way and after a few months we were forced to move to KLIA, about thirty-five miles away. Our offices there were right down by the apron, beyond security and a dirty twenty-minute walk from the terminal. Kathleen Tan, who I'd lured from Warner Singapore, was shocked that her designer shoes had to battle through oil spills, mud and mounds of rubbish on her way to work. This wasn't the first-class jet-set lifestyle of Warner Music and Kathleen, whose previous job had been in high-end fashion, was surprised at how basic all the facilities were.

With the new plane, we expanded our operations. We put on four flights to Penang – one of Malaysia's most important business and cultural hubs – and were looking at lots of new destinations. At first the passenger loads to Penang were low but we adjusted and began to make progress through trial and error.

When AirAsia started, the average member of the public just did not fly. There was a small percentage – say 10 per cent or 15 per cent of the population – who used MAS or Singapore Airlines a lot, but for the rest it would never have crossed their minds to get on a plane. We were creating a new market of fliers – but these people were often quite literally first-time fliers who had no idea what to do.

Bo Lingam, my operations director, who I'd also dragged over from Warner, tells a great story. One evening at about 5.00 p.m. he was walking through the landside seating area of the Subang terminal when he saw an old couple sitting with their suitcases in what was called the Waiting Area. He thought nothing of it and carried on with his end-of-day rounds, checking on staff and ground crew. He walked back through a couple of hours later and they were still sitting there with their cases. At that stage, AirAsia was about the only operator left at the airport, everyone else had moved to KLIA, so Bo walked over and said, 'Are you OK? Are you waiting for somebody?'

'No, we're waiting for our flight.'

'When's your flight?'

'We're not sure, we're just waiting here . . .'

It turns out that the flight had left at 7.00 a.m. They had bought tickets, made their way to the airport and sat down in the Waiting Area, almost as if at a bus stop, thinking that a plane would just appear and pick them up.

Bo of course arranged for them to fly on the next available flight and showed them what to do. These kinds of stories appeared almost daily so we commissioned a cartoonist to produce a comic to explain how to navigate the processes from the terminal doors to the seat on the aircraft. We weren't just opening up a new market and providing a new way to travel, we were educating a great part of the population on how to fly.

The slogan 'Now Everyone Can Fly' had come to me early on. As with many good ideas, it came in the shower one morning as I was thinking about what made our 'offer' to this new market special; what marked us out from the established airlines. The simplicity and boldness of the statement appealed to me – and, after all, with the fares we were offering, no one could really dispute it. When these stories started to come in, I felt we really were making good on our claim.

The energy from getting through the bird strike crisis propelled us through 2002, and we added three more planes over the course of the year. Within seven months we had wiped out our portion of the MYR 40 million debt. Again we felt we were making progress. We added new routes and continued to expand.

By November 2002 I thought we were on a pretty solid footing. I should have known that as soon as I had that feeling, it was time to worry. We had six planes, increasing passenger loads and were negotiating new routes. Our staff were loyal and constantly humbling in their dedication. It was at this point that I decided to call them 'Allstars' and every day they earn the title. I wanted to start flying internationally – Thailand, Singapore, Indonesia – and to open up South East Asia to our airline. But the World Health Organization – my dad's old employer – had other ideas. Or rather their announcement that a new disease called SARS was spreading through the region threw the airline industry into chaos.

SARS (severe acute respiratory syndrome) was first spotted in China at the end of 2002 and the WHO told the world about it in February 2003. The disease spread by human contact – usually when someone infected coughed or sneezed and saliva or mucus landed on someone else. Confining people in aircraft cabins was one of the worst things that could be done. The best prevention was to make sure that no one with the disease got on the plane. Globally, the media went mad. SARS was on every front page and led news programmes. In South East Asia a lot of airlines retreated from the crisis, cutting back on their operations and advertising.

I felt we should do the opposite. The WHO and governments in the region were putting measures in place to prevent transmission and it really wasn't our responsibility to manage that. My feeling was that in a crisis you should move aggressively because there are opportunities and gaps to fill. I went to my marketing and finance departments and told them to triple our advertising. Most financial controllers will cut brand advertising during a crisis, but it's actually the worst thing to do.

The reaction was as I expected: 'Are you mad? No one's flying!'

'Trust me,' I said, 'I know Malaysians. If you offer a low enough fare, they'll fly regardless of the risks. No one will fly to Kota Kinabalu for MYR 400 if they think they could die, but if you offer it at MYR 40, they won't care!'

We churned out the ads and the take-up was amazing. When the crisis abated, we were bigger and stronger and our reputation as an airline that operated in all circumstances was enhanced. People always need to fly and we wanted to make sure that they knew AirAsia would be there to help them. After all, our slogan promised exactly that.

We'd weathered 9/11, the bird strike and then SARS. Our first eighteen months had tested our resilience, our business model and our culture. I felt that we had passed with flying colours. The fleet stood at thirteen planes by the end of 2003.

Proof that our reputation was spreading came in the form of a phone call from an aide to the Thai Prime Minister, Thaksin Shinawatra. The aide told me that Thaksin was impressed with what we were doing and wanted to start a low-cost airline in Thailand. I leapt at the opportunity to build our brand and our network. We partnered with the Shin Corporation to establish AirAsia Thailand and I dragged in my old Warner colleague Tassapon Bijleveld to head up the new airline. I packed Bo Lingam off to help Tassapon set it up. It felt like a further vindication.

In January 2004, just after the region was picking itself up after SARS, reports started emerging of a new strain of bird flu in Vietnam and Thailand, and within weeks ten more countries had reported infection. It was, again, a global crisis over which we had no control. Panic set in amongst many airlines but, once more, I took the view that if others were retreating we should expand.

We announced an IPO in 2004 and couldn't seem to get anyone interested. I went knocking on every bank's door but was brushed off. Our fortunes changed when Credit Suisse saw the potential of our operation – particularly the possibility of taking over MAS's domestic routes, which I'd hinted might be in the offing – and were joined by a German bank (DVB). At the end of the process AirAsia was valued at $100 million – a staggering number given our starting point – and we sold 30 per cent of the available shares to a portfolio of investors to take us to the next level. The injection of cash made a massive difference – we'd been living cash-in-hand ever since our first flight.

Our use of technology was so important in the early days. As a way of maximizing what we got from each ticket sale, we were one of the first to move ticket sales online so that we didn't have to sell through travel agents and pay their commission. We sold tickets as far in advance as possible; got passengers to pay up front to ensure that our cash flow was as high as possible and made the tickets non-refundable. Even so, it was a hand-to-mouth existence before the IPO.

The injection of cash also woke our competitors up. MAS suddenly announced in 2004 that they were slashing their domestic fares to compete with or undercut ours. It was a devastating blow. Remember, they were subsidized by the government so the risk to them was minimal; whereas for us, every ringgit was life and death. So I went bananas. I still knew no one in the financial or aviation press but I had contacts on the music side and some of them had moved up to become overall editors. One of them, Datuk Ahirudin bin Attan, also known as Rocky Bru, had become editor of the *Malay Mail* and he wrote a front-page editorial saying that MAS were killing competition. It got our message out there and helped mobilize our support.

I also took the direct route. I gatecrashed a party where the transport minister was trying to enjoy himself. I think he stopped having such a good time when he saw me. I managed to persuade him that their campaign was unfair and he agreed to put a temporary halt to it. Hostilities were out in the open now, though.

The campaign put me in the role of a kind of Robin Hood. The message from the beginning of AirAsia had

With my adoring mum in Kuala Lumpur, 1965, when I was about one.

Even as a toddler I liked to party.

My dad and I in London in 1976 when I was twelve. We were on our way to visit Epsom College for the first time.

June 1993. A very proud dad to newborn Stephanie.

(1980: Rugby Junior Colts, Epsom College.) Football was always my game but I eventually grew to love rugby. I was fast and played on the wing.
(Epsom College Archive)

(1981: First XI hockey, Epsom College.) I loved hockey and was the youngest pupil to play for the First XI. My 'Vampire' stick was a treasured memento, autographed by the Indian World Cup team.
(Epsom College Archive)

(1983: Holman House, Epsom College.) Proudly sitting as House Captain. Holman were seen as mavericks by the rest of the school. And their colour was red.
(Epsom College Archive)

One of AirAsia's very first flights. I look like I don't quite believe I own the airline!

(AirAsia)

As CEO of an airline, I make sure I do all the jobs my staff do on a regular rotation – including loading suitcases on to the plane. I learn so much about what's really going on because of this.

(AirAsia)

This ad ran in the AirAsia Annual Report 2012–16. Long-term, trusting partnerships are vital in business. AirAsia and Credit Suisse have been working together profitably from our very earliest days.

(AirAsia)

How did Tony's dream take off?

How to turn a single dollar into Asia's largest low cost carrier. Tony Fernandes and Credit Suisse's Helman Sitohang explain how it's done at credit-suisse.com/apac

Enjoying Richard Branson serving me dinner en route from Perth to Kuala Lumpur after I had won a Formula One bet against him. To his eternal credit, Richard really got into the spirit of it. 13 May 2013 was a great day.

(AirAsia)

Proud co-owners watching our team. Din and I are more like brothers than business partners.
(Javier Garcia/Back Page Images)

24 May 2014. One of the greatest moments of my life. Celebrating with QPR fans after winning promotion against Derby at Wembley.

(Javier Garcia/Back Page Images)

9 July 2012. Ji-sung Park was a legend in Asia so signing him to play at QPR was a massive moment for me.

(Javier Garcia/Back Page Images)

Hugging our goalkeeper Robert Green after the amazing play-off final against Derby, 24 May 2014.

(Javier Garcia/Back Page Images)

Celebrating promotion on the Wembley pitch, 24 May 2014. Joey Barton didn't quite realize what he was taking on when he put me on his shoulders. Fair play though – he didn't drop me.

(Javier Garcia/Back Page Images)

A sign on the sixth floor of RedQ, AirAsia's headquarters. It reminds us every day to remember our roots. This is a favourite sign of Din's.　　　　　　　　　*(AirAsia)*

(RedQ, Kuala Lumpur International Airport.) There are no offices and all the meeting rooms have glass walls. We are an open organization.　　　　　*(AirAsia)*

been that we were on the passengers' side – that we would do everything we could to get them where they wanted to go. With that increasing reputation, the government found it hard to allow MAS to try to kill us because it would have been so unpopular with the voters.

This was brought home to me clearly when a little while after the MAS skirmish, I was asked by the Prime Minister to present to the National Economic Council. I hadn't seen him since that meeting when he'd granted us a licence but not fully opened the door. I walked into the room and everyone was miserable as hell – I think they were doing it to intimidate me. I just about got through the presentation.

After a long pause, Mahathir said, 'You should be congratulated, it's amazing what you've done.'

The whole mood of the room changed from intimidation to warm embrace.

The fallout from the presentation also boosted our cause. The PM removed the subsidy that MAS were paid on domestic routes. It was a huge moment because from that point on MAS had to compete with us on level ground – something they just weren't geared up to do. The situation was starting to become a little bit more like Goliath versus Goliath rather than David versus Goliath. Once again, I felt we were making real progress. The airline was growing fast, we had our first joint venture airline with AirAsia Thailand, had acquired a 49 per cent stake in the failing Awair Airline in Indonesia, and we had won a partial victory against the state-run MAS's monopoly on domestic routes. Our fleet was expanding and, thanks to our total focus on cost and aggressive marketing, we had cleared our portion of the debt we had taken on in 2001.

I was in my flat in London at Christmas 2004 when the first reports of the tsunami started to appear on the news. I watched in horror as the pictures showed whole villages swept away. An AirAsia plane was almost washed off the apron in Phuket. Immediately we got on top of the situation – offering to fly rescue and relief workers to the affected areas, providing as much information and logistical support as we could. We realized that the region would need a massive amount of support so we started the 'Love Phuket' campaign and made it a point of principle that we didn't cancel a flight.

When the scenes of devastation in Banda Aceh in Indonesia were broadcast, I arranged for us to fly there. Everyone thought I was mad but I repeated, 'We have to connect this community, we can't have them ostracized or cut off by this tragedy.'

I knew people had to get there to fix it as well, of course. I went to Aceh shortly after. I've seen a lot of things and been through some stressful and distressing situations but Banda Aceh was something else. It was flattened; not even Hollywood could have invented something as tragic. Every dwelling, house and high-rise had been ripped from its foundations, there were ships (not just boats) in the middle of the streets and the people were left with absolutely nothing except what they had on their backs. It was devastated and devastating.

Our links with Banda Aceh, I'm proud to say, are as strong now as they were back then. My commitment to the region means that I feel responsible and want to help wherever I can – to try to make something positive out of adversity.

AirAsia started to grow stronger. We took on more planes, our operations became slicker and our profile higher. We were making progress financially and, as far as market share was concerned, we were also, we thought, getting smarter at running the business.

We gained so much confidence that we took on sponsorship of one of the world's largest sports teams. In 2005, Manchester United FC approached us to sponsor their cafe. I'll admit I was a bit surprised – why would one of the biggest football clubs in the world be interested in a small Asian airline? But I knew a partnership would make sense for AirAsia – Manchester United's chief, David Gill, estimated that there were 40 million club fans in Asia so I definitely wanted to be involved. However, the cafe idea seemed a bit under-powered, so I said to David: 'No, I want to sponsor the club.'

David replied, 'Let's talk.'

I flew to London and met a guy called Andy Anson who had just been appointed Man United's commercial director. We signed an initial one-year deal which meant that we got our logo on the electronic pitch-side billboards.

It's difficult to express what a huge deal this was. We still only had a tiny fleet at the time, and going to Old Trafford, Din and I were like village boys – we didn't watch the match at all, we just looked out for when our logo would appear on the billboards.

The benefits worked both ways. Sir Alex Ferguson told me that the AirAsia sponsorship photo was the only one that the entire squad turned up for: football players like beautiful women and we had those by the plane-load. (We have beautiful men too, but the players tend to be less interested in them.) We painted the Man United crest on some tailfins and had portraits of players on the fuselage. One – with Rio Ferdinand, Alex Ferguson and Ji-sung Park – I remember particularly because Park later ended up at QPR for a season.

We handled the activation of the deal – the crucial part of any sponsorship – seamlessly, putting together a rolling programme of events that squeezed the most out of the association. Over and above the plane-painting, we ran competitions for Asian children to win a trial, flew a plane full of competition winners to Manchester to watch a game, sold Man United merchandise on the planes, and the players even came out to Kuala Lumpur. We set the trend for other Asian airlines who followed. Once again, being first made a difference: the team have such a huge following in Asia that our brand benefited immeasurably from the association. And Din and I got to meet and hang out with legends like Bobby Charlton, Sir Alex Ferguson and Wayne Rooney. The deal ran for three years, giving me a first taste of the football world.

Then in 2007–8 the financial crisis hit Wall Street and the global markets, and we were badly exposed by some hedged investments we'd made – at the banks' behest – on the oil price. Prior to the crash, the price was going up and up and up and killing all the airlines, so we took hedged positions to try to control our exposure. When the global crisis hit, the price plummeted, and it wiped out all our cash – MYR 1 billion. We were down to MYR 5–10 million, which wasn't far off where we started in 2001. A renewed intense focus on cost, aggressive marketing and the discipline to get back to our frugal early-days behaviour meant that within two years we were back to having 1 billion cash.

Since then I avoid the derivatives game – it is are a nightmare. My outlook has become highly risk averse. If I hedge, it is only for a year and I fix all interest rates and exchange rates where I can. Some companies take on derivatives trading, but to my mind, you might as well take the company cash to the casino. If you know which way the price of oil is going, you don't need to hedge, simple as that; if you don't know, you're as likely to come out on top as if you were to throw dice. Avoid gambling the company cash at all costs. For AirAsia it was a nearly fatal mistake.

We fought hard on every front. Persistence is one of my greatest strengths and probably one of my most annoying characteristics as far as my competitors are concerned. Getting routes out of MAS's hands has never been easy and it took seven years to be able to fly direct to Singapore. In the early days, I was blocked continually by the government so we decided we'd fly to Johor in southern Malaysia – which is about a forty-minute bus ride from Singapore – and take our passengers over the border. We launched the route and on the first day, when the disembarked passengers reached the Singapore border, the bus was impounded and the passengers dumped on the tarmac. We couldn't get them in – that was the level of opposition we faced from the Singapore government.

So it was a happy moment in 2008 when the first

AirAsia flight landed at Changi Singapore Airport. If you believe in something, you have to go all-in and see it through.

Unpredictability is part of the reason I love business and is a common theme in the AirAsia story. In spite of the many unforeseen problems, by 2012 we were a real force in Asian aviation: we had grown to a fleet of 118 planes and had carried nearly 20 million passengers. The pace of growth left a lot of competitors in our wake and the 'big boys' were starting to worry.

Nazir Razak (or Jay as I call him), the chairman of CIMB bank, came to see me in 2012 suggesting a deal that, if he'd proposed it ten years earlier, I'd have thought he was taking the piss but really, really badly. The CEO of MAS, Idris Jala, had been to see him and suggested that the three of us explore the possibility of a merger. My reaction is unprintable but let's just say I was at once excited and feeling pleased for us – we had come so far that the national carrier wanted to join forces. This was a major victory.

Of course, on paper it made absolute sense. MAS was struggling and they had been for a number of years. They had been owned by a private individual in the nineties who had made a mess of it to the point that the government had to step in and buy it back. Funnily enough, the individual had no airline experience either – but in this case he couldn't make it work. Even when we were setting up AirAsia, MAS had been knocking on the Prime Minister's door for a refinancing package to secure the airline's future.

Idris then relinquished the reins of MAS to become a cabinet minister. The government in principle still liked the idea of a merger but there was some nervousness I think about me running both companies. Instead of a merger, the idea changed to become a share swap – in effect, we'd get a piece of MAS and the government would have an interest in AirAsia. The main thrust of the deal was to increase efficiency in the domestic market. But the government were also at that time setting up the Malaysia Competition Commission (MyCC) to ensure there was free and fair competition in commercial markets in order to protect the consumer. The thought that MAS and AirAsia could be collaborating was contrary to the spirit and potentially to the practice of this new commission. So we faced a big problem there.

We also faced a classic problem: the outright hostility between the two airlines. I'm very open to working together to make things better for the consumer – AirAsia is built on the principle of providing a service for everyone, after all. However, our advertising and publicity battles with MAS had been brutal and our staffs would have had to swallow a lot of pride to start to work together, even if it was for the wider benefit of passengers.

If, as was being proposed, I was to run both companies, the atmosphere at board level would have been sour, and every collaborative initiative would have been treated with suspicion by MAS employees. We got to the stage where Din and I sat on the board of MAS and MAS had representatives at AirAsia board meetings. It was tricky – if MAS raised their fares, it was my fault; if AirAsia cut a route, it was my fault. I couldn't win and would always be seen as the wolf in the sheep pen as far as MAS were concerned.

So the political pressure groups and unions went to work to try to undo the arrangement. Jay told me that the Prime Minister in the end said that the deal was economically sound but a political minefield.

Finally the government decided to unwind the deal. It was a shame because there were already economies of scale, and the benefits of sharing resources were starting to emerge, but it couldn't be sustained. For us it was an opportunity that didn't quite work out, but for MAS it was more than that. After the whole deal fell apart, they had to go through a massive restructuring which led to thousands of job losses.

It was frustrating but, as far as AirAsia was concerned, still a milestone: the national full-service carrier would have merged with us if the political climate had been right. That in itself was highly significant.

They say that the strongest metals are forged in the hottest fires and for AirAsia those crises in our infant years generated a lot of heat. Each time we got hit by a disaster we emerged stronger. We did that by aggressively facing up to the challenge rather than backing down. As long as safety is not compromised, I feel that crisis brings opportunity. Would I have started the airline if I'd known what we'd be hit with in the first six years? I'd like to think I would. We worked incredibly hard, and there were some low moments, but at the end of it we felt in pretty good shape. From an airline with just two aircraft, a handful of routes, a monthly deficit of MYR 4 million and no future, in just twelve years we had built an award-winning, low-cost airline that operated 158 planes on 182 routes, carrying 42.6 million passengers and generating MYR 5.11 billion. We had joint venture partners in Thailand, Indonesia and the Philippines, and had started a long-haul operation, AirAsia X. And we felt we had a reputation as a reliable, great value, low-cost airline.

At the end of 2013, I was asked by a journalist what I had left to fear, given all that we'd been through. I replied that I feared the unknown. The unknown was about to appear.

7. Tragedy Strikes

Soundtrack: 'Tears Falling Down on Me' by Carole King

The phone rang at 8.25 a.m. on 28 December 2014. I was standing in the bathroom of my home in Kuala Lumpur preparing for a day out with my children, Steph and Stephen. We'd had a lovely Christmas and I'd promised a shopping trip to round off the holidays.

I picked the phone up.

'Tony, it's Bo.'

My heart started to race. Bo Lingam only ever calls if something is seriously wrong.

'An AirAsia Indonesia Airbus has disappeared from the radar . . .'

'What? When? Where was it flying to?'

'Tony, all I've got so far is that it was flying to Singapore from Surabaya, it took off at 5.35 a.m. and the last contact was 6.18 a.m. I just got the call from Adrian.'

Adrian Jenkins, as I mentioned before, is my group director of Flight Operations and one of our most experienced pilots. He had called Bo to alert him to the potential problem. They were both on their way to our offices at the airport.

My reaction was physical: my mouth went dry, my stomach flipped and I reached out to the wall to support myself. I knew this wasn't a training exercise – something in my gut, my blood, somewhere, knew this was a real emergency.

We quickly agreed that I should join them at KLIA. I got in the car and called Din, who was, at it happened, in Singapore. He went straight to the airport to liaise with the authorities and to see what he could do. If our worst fears were realized there would be a lot of families arriving at the airport soon and he would have to help coordinate our response.

As I drove, the sense of dread built. It had been a tragic year for aviation in the region. In March, MH370 – an MAS flight en route from Kuala Lumpur to Beijing – had gone down without a trace; 239 souls had perished. Then in July an MAS flight had been downed over eastern Ukraine while flying from Amsterdam to Kuala Lumpur. The death toll was 298. We at AirAsia had felt those losses as keenly as everyone else in the region and had offered whatever help we could to MAS at the time.

There had been false alarms for AirAsia before – once I was going into a meeting with the Prime Minister when Bo called me and said that we'd lost contact with a plane in Indonesia. I had those same physical symptoms but had to carry on with the meeting. About halfway through, the PM asked me whether I was OK and I could only mumble, 'Yes, fine,' just wanting the meeting to end – despite the fact that we'd been waiting months for it. When I could finally escape, I called Bo back and it was a false alarm – a training routine that the CAA (Civil Aviation Authority) instigated randomly. I was so angry I wanted to start chucking things out of the window.

Another time I was in London and someone sent out a press release saying that we'd lost a plane. They hadn't warned me that it was a training exercise. My heart had stopped. Again.

I arrived at the same time as Adrian and we went in together. Some people were already there and more were arriving by the second, everyone with a look of disbelief on their faces. We met in the crisis room – it wasn't a room I'd been in before. In fact, I'd not been through any of the crisis training that some of the others had.

When I walked in, it was pretty clear that the aircraft was gone.

There was a lot of debate about whether I should go out to Indonesia or stay put and let the Indonesians handle it. It wasn't really a debate in my mind. I didn't care what the lawyers or the Indonesian government or whoever else said, I had to go out there. The reasons were simple: I had to be there because my staff had been killed and I had to be there for the families of the passengers. I wasn't prepared to hide behind a shield of lawyers. So I flew out to Surabaya. All the way through the flight I was tweeting updates or information, and messages of support and sympathy. Many of the messages were for the staff because I knew they would be hurting badly.

I didn't realize that a lot of the tweets were being broadcast by BBC and CNN and going global. To me, they were personal messages for people I knew in some cases, the cabin crew, and for everyone affected by what had happened – the families of the passengers – and all of the AirAsia family. In other words, there was no PR agency or strategy, and there was certainly no attempt to make a distinction between an Indonesian flight and a Malaysian one as some lawyers had suggested I make. This was an AirAsia tragedy and it affected us all.

That flight to Surabaya was the longest of my life. I sat in the cabin and turned over and over in my mind what I could possibly say. Of course, we didn't yet know what had happened and so speculation of any kind was futile. In the end I didn't have to prepare anything, I just spoke from the heart. I tried to share my grief, tried to send as much support as I could to the families and to my staff who were all suffering as much as I was. And I was publicly grateful to airlines, the government, the rescue agencies and anyone else who offered support either physical or emotional. Dealing with this kind of tragedy has to be from the heart – no scripted comments or rehearsed lines can be as effective.

When I arrived in Surabaya I couldn't believe the sheer number of cameras, reporters, TV crew, onlookers. It was overwhelming. In the background I could hear people saying, 'Tony's here, Tony's here,' as I walked into the crisis room at the airport that the authorities had set up for the families.

Their faces brought home to me the scale of what was happening. I realized I'd let them all down – what could I possibly say to make the pain go away? There were 155 passengers on QZ8501 and a lot of their families were packed into the room, desperate for any news. The Indonesian authorities were handling the situation, but all in the Indonesian language, so I couldn't help there. I was just standing by until one of the family members shouted, 'The face of the brand is here. I want to hear from him.'

So then I spoke and people asked me questions. I either didn't know the answers or just had partial answers, but I promised to find out what I could and keep them up to date with whatever new information emerged. After that, I did a live press conference with the Indonesian minister of transportation which went out globally.

Then I went back into the room and met every single family. The questions were full of desperation and hope:

'Could they be in a life raft?'

'Could they have made it on to an island?'

'Could they have somehow survived the crash anyhow?'

In my heart, I knew they'd gone but I did try to maintain the hope that they might have survived until we had definite proof either way. Reports started to come in of some of the aircraft parts being found and we began briefly to hope there had been a soft landing and that maybe some people had survived, but then I saw the transport minister alone and he told me that the plane had come down very fast. They could see from the radar that it had spun and descended too quickly. At that point, I gave up hope that anyone had survived.

And then your mind flits briefly to blame – no one wants it to be their fault. We knew the plane was flying in bad weather and it was a strong possibility that might be a main factor in the crash. But there were lots of factors – and the airline had to be counted as one of them.

The passengers' families were gentle and kind. One older lady who had lost a lot of her family members started hitting me, but she was an exception. Her family calmed her down and apologized but I was never going to complain about that kind of reaction – it was entirely understandable. I gave my phone number to everyone and stayed in touch. I'm still in touch with some of the families, as it happens. At the time I remember thinking that the only thing I could offer was good communication. I couldn't rescue their loved ones or bring them back to life, all I could do was be there and answer whatever questions they had. The families seemed to appreciate that. So I just talked and talked and talked to them – sitting for hours. Din was doing the same with the families in Singapore. I said at a press conference, 'It is probably an airline CEO's worst nightmare. After thirteen years of flying millions of people, it is the worst feeling one could have, but we stay strong for the families out there to make sure we can look after them even after the incident. We want to keep in contact with [victims' families] so we can provide the necessary support they may require.'

We appointed a care provider from AirAsia to each of the families.

The staff were next on my list. I visited the AirAsia Indonesia offices to reassure and comfort them – the company is like a family and the tragedy was not just about the passengers, it was about the loss of friends and colleagues in a close-knit group. This applied to all AirAsia, not just the Indonesian company.

After the first day in Surabaya I went back to my hotel room, drained and in a daze. The room seemed so empty. I didn't really sleep but somehow I found the strength to go back the next day and the next and the one after that. All the while I was getting messages from the families. Some touched me very deeply. Several weeks after I'd left Surabaya I was talking to Jenny Wakana, our communications head, and asked her to scroll through some of the messages. She hadn't known I was talking direct to the families. She dug out one exchange which she wanted to share with the company. The family member was happy for her to do it and I felt it would help the staff understand that the families weren't blaming AirAsia completely for the loss of their loved ones.

She sent out the following email on my behalf:

Allstars,

Over the past few weeks, I have been in touch with many of the family members and loved ones of our guests and crew onboard QZ8501, trying to offer as much support as I can.

Meeting and speaking with the family members and getting to know their stories has been heartbreaking and humbling and yet it's given me the resolve to want to make this truly the world's best, safest airline, together with all of you.

Here's a conversation I had with one of the family members that I want to share:

12 Jan 19:25 – QZ8501: Tony stay strong, i'm one of family members who got accident with airasia. I lost 2 my lovely sisters in these accident, you can buy plane again even if you should work hard from the low level again my be, but i dont have anything to make my sisters live again except my Jesus do some miracle. But i appreciated your responsibility as CEO Airasia, i hope your crew and managemet learn from you. Also I hope these accident is not human error because if its true it would be hurt for us who lost our belove family. But i support you too as personal, i know that you are great CEO through these very hard time. keep humble, you try to do the best to make our family member pass these sorrow, really appreciated. Tony keep moving and pls make everyone SAFE to fly GBU

12 Jan 19:28 – QZ8501: Because in this time too i really scary to get flight, even my job push me to keep flying every month. Through this accident maybe not only i lost my sisters but also my job. Please promise to me make everyone SAFE to fly

12 Jan 20:30 – Tony Airasia Fernandes: Thank you for you lovely note. What is your name. I'm so sorry about your loss. My heart bleeds. I'm determined to make Airasia the safest airline. I will share your note with all my staff. To ensure we get better. Don't be scared to fly. We can help you overcome your fear. Don't be afraid. I will fly with you. I hope your sisters are in a better place. I'm so so sorry. Pls give me your contact.

12 Jan 21:16 – QZ8501: It's ok Tony, i try to let my sisters Go. Just cascade to your crew keep make everyone fly i love these idea too but please make it safe too, i know thats would bring joy to everyone who have dream to see another country with low cost budget like me, my sister and whole family. Keep your dream and make it true.

12 Jan 23:54 – Tony Airasia Fernandes: Felly I'm really sorry

13 Jan 00:01 – QZ8501: Maybe it's not your false but may it will be lesson for learned for every airasia member, i wish all of you will be better Tony, i know it hurt u too and all of your crew

13 Jan 00:02 – Tony Airasia Fernandes: For 13 years we never had an accident

13 Jan 00:02 – Tony Airasia Fernandes: Never. We carried 250 million people

13 Jan 00:02 – Tony Airasia Fernandes: I never believed it would happen

13 Jan 00:13 – QZ8501: Yes tony thats why me, my whole family love to use airasia. The first maskapai [airline] which brought me to overseas. Your maskapai make my dream come true

13 Jan 00:13 – QZ8501: I trust your safety profile

13 Jan 00:13 – QZ8501: But now even with others maskapai im really scary to fly

13 Jan 00:14 – QZ8501: Its ok

13 Jan 00:14 – QZ8501: Lets learn and overcome these situation

13 Jan 00:14 – QZ8501: Even my dady

13 Jan 00:14 – QZ8501: He forgive the accident

13 Jan 00:14 – QZ8501: He said you are great CEO

13 Jan 00:15 – QZ8501: Keep moving Tony

13 Jan 00:15 – QZ8501: I just want to said these because i know u try ur best

13 Jan 00:15 – QZ8501: I love your dream in airasia

13 Jan 00:16 – QZ8501: And i know this time you have a lot of complain from many passanger family who very sad with these accident

13 Jan 00:16 – QZ8501: But i hope you never stop with these make everyone can fly

13 Jan 00:17 – QZ8501: Because my dream to see another country comes true because of that

13 Jan 00:17 – QZ8501: Too

I know it's tough. But we must not give up. We owe it to all of those we lost to live up to our promise of 'now everyone can fly' and help dreams come true.

Let us work harder, be diligent and smile brighter for our guests. Safety is a marathon – we need to continuously improve and learn every day.

Together, we will be the world's best again, as we always have been.

Love,
Tony

*

A Singapore submarine found the aircraft on 7 January, and pictures emerged of flight 8501 sitting on the bottom of the sea. The first emotion was, honestly, a sense of relief: relief that the desperate search was over; relief that there was some closure for the victims' families and relief that we could start to help them through the next stage of grieving. And then there was deep sadness when the pictures of the tail fin with our livery being lifted out of the sea were broadcast around the world. I also felt deeply for the victims of the MAS flight 370 who still don't have the physical evidence of what happened to their loved ones.

The first body was discovered – it was one of the cabin crew, Hayati Lutfiah Hamid – and I went to her funeral. I collected the body from Surabaya and took it to her home town for the funeral. It turned into a media scrum and some people said that it was insensitive of me to attend, but the family were thrilled with the attention – they said their daughter always wanted to be a star. And their religion helped support them through the loss.

Din and I went to passenger funerals too. Din is religious and I think his belief gave him strength, which helped me too. We're both emotional people and could not hide our feelings even if we had wanted to. Instead, we made it clear how much we were hurting and, in a curious way, that helped us get through this nightmare not as badly scarred as we might have been.

When the dust settled, there was still an airline to run. There was still a responsibility to the staff and passengers to provide a safe and secure means of transport. AirAsia came out of the tragedy in reasonable standing with the public, I think. We handled the crisis in the best possible way we could; and the only way we knew was by being open, honest and natural. There weren't any corporate shields or faceless PR people and we didn't hide behind the government investigators. We fronted up and I think the public responded to that.

I realized during and after the crisis that you really see the strength of a person when things are bad. Nowadays we talk about 'One AirAsia' and back then we really had it – the whole company pulling together and showing their strength. We had guys in the care provider teams who were with the victims' families for sixty or seventy days without seeing their own families. They cared deeply and genuinely, and to me, as CEO and founder of this company, nothing could make me prouder than the way we as a group responded to this unspeakable tragedy. Everyone from everywhere in AirAsia came down to Indonesia to help however they could. It was one of the proudest moments in AirAsia that everyone in the company responded in such an admirable way – by being genuine and caring and doing the right thing. It didn't matter whether they were Muslim, Catholic, Malaysian, Indonesian, Thai or Japanese – everyone put effort in. The public saw and appreciated that.

We suspended marketing activities for a month in all the areas except Indonesia, where we stayed offline for about two months.

No airline can ever say it's 100 per cent safe. Safety is a never-ending race – you've got to keep getting better and staying ahead of potential problems. There are always things you can explore to see if there are better methods or standards; and every day you have to be vigilant, thorough and professional to ensure safety is always top of the list.

I was perhaps a little remote from AirAsia before the accident because I'd been involved with Formula One, QPR and Tune, the umbrella company of Din and my other interests. As a result of the crash and its consequences, I got stuck back in and for the past two years I've been aggressively hands-on in the way that I run the business. There was talk in the aftermath of the crash of closing AirAsia Indonesia, but I disagreed – and now it's doing well.

The number of tears we shed though was incredible;

funerals, meetings, discovery of plane parts – whatever the occasion, we felt it all the way through us.

Someone said to me recently that nothing has come easy to AirAsia and it's true. Everything that we've achieved, we've achieved through blood, sweat and tears. There have been no straight paths. We got through the daunting task of setting up the airline and started flying: our fleet was halved by a bird strike. We got through the bird strike, SARS and bird flu, and then the Bali bomb of 2005 hit the region and threw all plans out of the window. We grew because of our aggressive strategy during these crises. Even when the world financial crisis hit, we worked doubly hard and came out ahead, only for the oil price to tank just after we'd taken a hedged position, which wiped out half of our cash; again we dragged ourselves through, but then the greatest tragedy of all befell us – QZ8501. We dedicated ourselves to the passengers' families, to reviewing and enhancing our safety record (which had been spotless) and then we were faced with a report in which perhaps, I felt, we shouldered more of the blame than we should have done. We learned and got better.

In the aftermath of the tragedy, I felt we needed to ensure that the highest possible standards were being maintained in every territory in which we operated. Each territory had a different mandatory standard of operational fitness. So we created a group structure for the airline, and we made sure that all our standards conformed to the highest requirements of the whole region.

What happened in one country affected the whole company and, as far as the outside world was concerned, the whole brand. And so out of this came the idea of 'One AirAsia', which is currently being implemented. We'll no longer have AirAsia Thailand, AirAsia Philippines and so on, it will simply be AirAsia whenever and wherever we fly. This is really important for the development of the airline as a whole. As the company gets bigger – we've grown from 250 staff to nearly 20,000 (with more to come) – it's imperative to hold on to the family identity and culture, so getting rid of regional tags is a significant help in bringing people together.

My philosophy throughout my business career is that you should always be transparent and honest. If you do something wrong, you hold your hand up, apologize, do what it takes to make it right and move on. This applies to tragedies as much as it does to smaller things. Recently I was alerted to an ad Tune Protect placed on the backs of some of AirAsia's aeroplane seats. The ad denigrated nurses, calling them 'lousy'. It was just a stupid ad that should never have got on to an AirAsia plane. When someone showed it to me, I immediately told the CEO to remove it, apologized unreservedly to the professional nurses' body and made a public statement acknowledging the mistake. Again, it was a case of holding your hand up, saying sorry and moving on.

From great tragedy to smaller annoyances, the only way to gain trust and enhance your reputation and to get better is to be open and truthful. Apparently, our handling of the loss of flight QZ8501 and the 167 passengers and crew has been the subject of some academic papers on 'Crisis Management'. In such tragic circumstances, you can only hope that some good will come of it; if AirAsia's reaction to the terrible, terrible loss of life is helpful to others then maybe that's a contribution. The communication routes and accessibility of our staff seem to be the key factors here. We deliberately made sure that we didn't hide behind a corporate or legal shield. Given there was little anyone could actually do to save the situation, the fact that we were as visible and as helpful as we could be gave at least a little comfort to the victims' grieving families.

8. The AirAsia Journey

Soundtrack: 'Come Fly with Me' by Frank Sinatra

On 7 November 2016, AirAsia opened the doors of its new corporate headquarters, RedQ, positioned by Kuala Lumpur International Airport's second terminal. It had been a bumpy long-haul flight from early 2001, when we crammed five people into my old Warner office, to this gleaming 18,000-square-metre six-storey building, home to 2,000 of AirAsia's 20,000 staff.

The space and design reflect my business philosophy. Everything is open plan or, if there are rooms with walls, they are glass. Nobody has an office. Diagonal walkways cross a wide and high atrium which makes for an airy, bright environment; there are free seating areas and a cafeteria that offers seven varieties of fresh food, all cooked in the building. The emphasis is on healthy eating. Facilities on site include a shop, a gym, automated teller machines and a coffee station, and we have a doctor and medical team; there are plans for a crèche and other amenities. We provide as much as possible at work so that our Allstars can get on and do their work with no fuss or distraction. RedQ looks out on to the apron where we can see our planes taxiing, taking off and landing, so we are reminded constantly what we're there to do. When we designed the building, we took staff suggestions seriously so that we could most effectively create an environment in which we knew everyone would work to their best. One of my greatest pleasures is walking into RedQ in the morning and hearing the noise of people enjoying their work.

The opening ceremony was an incredible moment for me. I feel RedQ represents the kind of organization we've matured into – one that has a prominent place in South East Asian enterprise. We are the brand that you see when your plane taxis into KLIA – just as easyJet was the brand I saw at Luton all those years ago.

With some fresh deals in the pipeline as I write this, I ultimately hope to achieve the dream of establishing an airline that operates in every major country and region in Asia, from India to China and Japan to Indonesia, the Philippines and Malaysia. We are pushing hard to become the number-one airline in all territories. Our growth has been phenomenal despite all of the setbacks. We are around 20,000 employees; our revenue is rocketing; our fleet is going to touch 500 by 2028. In June 2017, I signed a deal with Airbus for an additional fourteen aircraft to be ready for 2018–19 because of the ticket demands we're experiencing. With that signature we became Airbus's number-one customer, outstripping Lufthansa and Emirates. AirAsia group will have purchased 688 aircraft from them since we started in 2001 at a value of over $90 billion.

In the same month, we were named the world's Best Low-Cost Carrier for the ninth year running. We are no longer the underdog or the Robin Hood of the aviation business. We are now a Goliath and becoming a Goliath brings a whole new set of challenges.

There's a poster up on the wall of the sixth floor of

RedQ which Din points to when he's talking to people about AirAsia. It says simply, 'Work hard. Stay humble.'

I reminded our senior management team of this at a conference we had in Phuket in 2017. The theme of the conference was future planning and culture. I wanted to restate to the senior team the story of our origins, our mission and our values because if we want to dominate the aviation business in Asia, we have to continue to act like David even though we are Goliath. How we do that was the essence of the conference. Culture, I said, was central to being able to achieve this.

How do you create and maintain the right culture to become the world beaters AirAsia has become? It comes from the people and from ways of doing and thinking.

One of the things we have always done is look inwards – we don't care about competitors. Our competitors are ourselves. The day our ego gets the better of us, the day we don't focus on costs, that's the day we have to worry. That's our competition, always. Our discipline of competing with ourselves on cost is fundamental to maintaining our place.

While a lot of companies focus on external branding, I believe that internal branding – what the staff think of the company, how they respond to the mission and strategy – is more important. If the staff understand, support and enhance your ideals, you're 50 per cent of the way there. Why try to sell your vision to outsiders if your staff don't get it? If they *do* get it, every single member of staff is a walking advertisement and endorsement. That's what we've been so good at and when it came to QZ8501 and the way our staff responded, I think you can see its value.

As I've said, creating an environment in which people

can express themselves is paramount. A lot of our best ideas come from the staff; this would be the case in most businesses but we have created a culture that encourages everyone to express those ideas. And it's vital that with the massive increase in staff – from 200 to 20,000 in sixteen years – there is the environment and platform to continue to allow that to happen.

Way back in 2004, Celia Lao Sio Wun (who was our first employee recruited in greater China and is now in charge of our operations in Hong Kong and Macau) suggested we fly to Macau. We were the first low-cost airline to do so. We've been going ever since and now operate four flights a day from Kuala Lumpur and more from other hubs.

Wherever I spend time within the AirAsia family I get suggestions and pick up ideas. For example, I went to the funeral of one of our Indian engineers, which was deeply moving. Afterwards, a mourning colleague told me about a destination called Tiruchirappalli, which I'd never heard of. I got our route planners to investigate and we're now flying there regularly. Again, we're one of the first to do it.

In the early days, I was talking to the chief engineer, who said that he thought we could extend the life of the aeroplane tyres if the pilots landed the aircraft in a slightly different way.

'Why don't you tell them?' I asked.

'Oh, I couldn't do that. Us engineers can't tell a pilot how to fly a plane,' he replied hesitantly.

'Well, that changes now,' I stated.

At the time, we only had six or seven planes and they'd all come back to Kuala Lumpur at the end of each day when the engineers would get to work on them overnight.

I used to call the pilots in to talk about the day gone and the day ahead. That night I left the chief engineer to talk to the pilots about his idea. At about midnight my PA, Kim, called me and said, 'I think you'd better come in. It's getting a bit hot in the meeting.'

I walked in and there was a lot of hostility in the room from the pilots. After hearing their concerns I said: 'Guys, it's for your own benefit.'

We increased the landings per set of wheels from 80 to 220. It was also the start of a close collaboration between the pilots and the engineers. That was the day I decided they should both have the same epaulettes on their shoulders – after all, without engineers, pilots wouldn't be able to fly.

If people are too scared to speak out, they won't come up with ideas and the company won't innovate. When a business isn't innovating, it will die. Just look at Nokia, BlackBerry or Kodak, who all stood still and suffered. A business has to evolve and the people are the drivers for change. How the company adapts and deals with change is critical.

We had been using Google+ as our intra-company communications platform since the early days but it wasn't really helping our Allstars get their ideas and messages out. It just wasn't up to it. One day I saw an article about Facebook's new platform for business communication, Facebook Workplace, in the *Wall Street Journal*. I was in touch with Facebook the next day and we had signed a deal to install it for all our staff within four days. We had 8,000 people talking to each other instantly. You have to innovate and, when you do, you have to move quickly. A lot of companies would have gone through a six-month evaluation process, got their technical teams, HR and representatives from each department to represent their voices, before finally making a decision. That's way too slow – paralysis by analysis once more. The whole idea loses momentum and focus and will probably be dead in the water before it's even launched.

I encourage my staff to tell me if they don't like something about the business – anything. That isn't to say that I'm going to agree every time but at least there is the platform and opportunity to say it without fear of the sack or censure in some way. Recently, I withdrew some flight coupons (AirAsia staff get heavily discounted flights on our routes) because they were being abused. I got a ton of messages complaining about it – people said they thought it was wrong or unfair or suggested a different way of tackling the problem. I listened to the ideas, engaged in the conversation, and as a collective group we reformed the policy in under six hours. I was proud of everyone at that point for two reasons: first, that they had the courage to stand up against something they believed wasn't right; and second, because the culture and environment meant they could do so without being scared.

Every manager, director and CEO says they have an open-door policy, but their door's always closed. We've abandoned doors altogether: offices are a major source of frustration and politics, which create barriers to communication. Having a working space where people can move around and talk to each other regardless of who they are is so important. Not enough modern leaders spend time simply walking around their workplaces; they sit there in ivory towers on the sixth or sixtieth floor and feel they are too important to mix. I spend half my time walking around, talking to people and asking questions about their family; establishing a rapport and listening. It gives everyone a sense of 'He knows what I do and he cares about it', which is vital for company loyalty and for a culture in which sharing is valued. I do the same whenever I take an AirAsia flight – I get up and say 'hello' to the passengers. You learn so much from everyone you talk to and they're sitting ducks for two hours – I urge my cabin crew to get as much information from every passenger as possible. The information is so much more useful than 1,000 customer feedback forms.

My style is different from most Asian management, which is rigidly hierarchical. Instead, I believe in democracy and that flat structures are the best way. My aim is that from top to bottom there should be only three layers; there shouldn't be multiple branches to the management tree. People should be allowed to get on with their jobs, becoming better and better at them. Too often, layers are created to appease people who want a better job title, but management have to concentrate on the work that's being done.

Hierarchy is one weight I've tried to reduce at AirAsia. Another is bureaucracy, which I think is possibly the biggest enemy of an organization. Facebook Workplace is a tool to combat this. Instead of sending out companywide emails from HR or the Comms team, anyone can upload a video, share a thought or chip in to a discussion. You have to have rules, particularly in a business like aviation, but within that framework you have to have freedom; bureaucracy kills a lot of creativity.

At the conference in Phuket, we talked a lot about getting back to the dynamic culture of our smaller, younger days. Too often I felt I'd seen people hiding behind spreadsheets or in meetings. Aviation is about providing a safe, cheap, enjoyable journey for passengers. You can't be a part of that if you sit in front of a laptop screen all day. I encouraged everyone to get out and fly as much as possible.

After sixteen years, there are three main things that I've learned about running businesses. Call it my business philosophy if you like.

1. A company must be able to adapt to change.
2. A company must be disruptive – it must create models that weren't there before.
3. A company must have the right people.

Where I've been less successful in the past is when one of those three things wasn't applied.

The future is now about moving AirAsia from 'just' an airline to a big-data technology company, because that's what I see as the next frontier. Data is the new oil and I want AirAsia not only to be the world's best low-cost airline every year in the future, I want it to be a data platform to drive other businesses. But that's for another chapter.

9. Ground Speed

Soundtrack: 'Fast Car' by Tracy Chapman

From the outside, my Formula One experience looks pretty shambolic: I ended up in court, created a team that didn't do well and in the process lost a lot of money. As a business venture, you'd mark it up as a disaster. But while all that is true, I actually think that F1 was good for me and for AirAsia, and if I was given the chance to do it again, I'd leap at it. I'd do it differently, admittedly – but I'd definitely do it.

A passion for racing reaches back to my childhood. As a kid, the highlight of my year was to go to the small racetrack at Batu Tiga with my dad, about half an hour in the car from Damansara Heights. We'd go for a full weekend, taking in all of the Formula Two and MotoGP races that were on the programme. The noise, the huge crowds, the edge of competition have all stayed with me.

When I came to England in 1977, my day-student friends would invite me to their homes on Sundays to watch the Grand Prix on TV. Later in my school career, I'd go to Brands Hatch and sit outside the circuit listening to the cars, spending the weekend there camping. I never had enough money to go into the track, but the thrill of being there on race weekends was enough.

My hero from the start was Frank Williams. He was also one of my tuck-box stickers.

Frank had started off as a driver and mechanic before moving on to designing and producing cars, initially in the Formula Two and Three classes. In 1977, the year I started at Epsom, he entered the Formula One championship, coming second in the constructors' championship in 1979 and then winning both the drivers' title with Alan Jones and the constructors' competition in 1980. Perhaps it is because his career coincided with the start of my new life at Epsom, or because he was so passionate about his profession, his cars, the drivers and the sport, but to me Frank Williams is a legend.

I have followed motor racing throughout my life. I cried when I went, with my family, to the first Malaysian Grand Prix in 1999 at the newly built Sepang International Circuit. Just hearing the rev of the Formula One engines and imagining what my dad would have made of a Grand Prix starting in Malaysia was enough to tip me over the edge. I went back as often as I could.

As has often happened in my life, one business I'm involved with takes me into new worlds and I've been lucky enough that the new world is one I'm passionately interested in. This was the case when AirAsia did the Manchester United sponsorship deal in 2005. When the press reported that we were thinking of that deal, Marcus Wight, who worked at the French advertising giant Havas, got in touch. We started to work together on the Man United deal – he and colleague Nick Lockwood helped the marketing team through the whole process and another important partnership was formed.

It was also the start of a relationship with the two of them that is still going strong today. When they decided to set up their own media and sponsorship company, called Phar, I encouraged them to grow their business in South East Asia. I always told them there was more to life than catching the same train every morning from a Surrey station. It has given me great pleasure to see Phar grow throughout the region over the years and one day I think I will help them take on Havas.

I'm unusual in the airline business because, with the exception of Richard Branson, I'm by nature a marketeer and a brand creator. A lot of airline CEOs are aviation experts but I've come at the business from a different angle and it's served me well. The Man United deal had been superb for our brand so Marcus, Nick and I started to explore other ideas.

Two thousand and seven was a good time to be a sponsor. There wasn't a lot of cash around for it because of the financial crash and Marcus and Nick got us increasingly good deals in the world of Formula One, starting with just the AirAsia logo on the driver's helmet, before we began to talk to Williams about a spot on the car itself.

As with any other deal, sponsorship for me is about the relationship with the partners. At the point that we were about to spend more with Williams, Din and I went to Oxfordshire in March 2007 to meet Frank Williams. Like I said, my life has been about making my dreams come true. If I'd known when I was fifteen I was going to write that sentence, I'd have pinched myself. The meeting was one of the biggest thrills of my life – the man was such an inspiration. Our sponsorship was a three-year deal for a small AirAsia flash on the Williams car but that wasn't really the point. Frank released a statement that was worth more than its weight in gold when we signed:

> We are immensely proud to have AirAsia as the latest addition to our partner portfolio. From a standing start, it now carries more passengers than Singapore Airlines in a matter of five years and is a very impressive organisation with clear global ambition. We look forward to assisting this ongoing international growth and, of course, to the team using AirAsia's services for the significant number of races we now attend in locations served by the airline.

The point about sponsorship is not the money you spend or the exposure you get from the placement of your logo, it's about making the association come alive for people – what sponsorship people call 'activation'. You have to plan and budget for this. Once you pay for the sponsorship itself you have to set aside the same amount of money to exploit and squeeze the association you have with Williams or Manchester United. Activation is the key to making any sponsorship deal work.

On 8 April 2007 I stood with the Williams team on the starting grid of the Sepang International Circuit wearing my red AirAsia cap. If my dad could have seen me, he would have been so proud. I wiped a tear away and looked around: 120,000 fans at the circuit with millions watching worldwide. Earlier that week the F1 team had flown into Kuala Lumpur on an AirAsia Airbus painted in the Williams colours, and it was broadcast live on TV: the activation was starting to pay off.

To be honest, I think I'd have been happy to keep going

with the Williams sponsorship deal. I got to go to a Grand Prix and hang out with incredible people like Frank Williams, Ron Dennis (the legend behind McLaren) and the drivers. AirAsia benefited from extraordinary exposure globally. The estimated worldwide television audience for Formula One in 2008 was 600 million viewers – no amount of lavish advertising, canny marketing or controversial PR can get you that kind of recognition. With all the side events and spin-offs we were able to run, the money invested was more than worth it.

But in June 2009, I was on my way to Ascot when my phone went.

'Tony, it's Déj.'

'Hello, my man. What's happening?'

'You know you like motor racing? A friend asked me whether you'd like to put an F1 bid together.'

'Hahaha.'

'I'm serious. There's an opening in the 2010 season – BMW has withdrawn so there's a slot, if you're interested.'

As always with life, if someone offers you an opportunity, the very least you can do is have a proper look at it.

I went to meet Max Mosley at Brands Hatch. First up, I asked him to tell me straight: how much did it cost to run a Formula One team? His answer was $40 million a year – less than previous years because the plan for the 2010 season was to place less emphasis on the technology and engineering, and to get back to racing. This appealed. It was still an eye-watering amount of money but the concept of pitting the drivers against each other rather than focusing on the size of engineering budgets meant that a new team would have more of a chance of getting at least the odd point. Din and I looked hard at the numbers and decided we still needed another partner. We called S. M. Nasarudin, who was CEO of the Naza Group, a conglomerate which mainly deals in car trading. He agreed to come in with us.

If we were going to do this we'd have to build a team and a car from scratch. As with AirAsia, we knew nothing about the business we were getting into. Our first port of call, after we'd met Max, was to talk to a man called Mike Gascoyne.

Mike's last job had been chief technology officer at Force India – previously known as Spyker – and before that he had worked at McLaren, Tyrrell, Jordan, Benetton/Renault and Toyota. Mike was being eased out of Force India, so he signed up as our technical director, which meant leading the design and build of our car.

Then we went for it. We had to put a bid together to present to the FIA (Fédération Internationale de l'Automobile), motor sport's governing body, and provide bank guarantees. Din and I looked after the money side and left the bid to the experts: Nino Judge, who had worked with Lotus for years, Sir Harry Nuttall, a sports marketing entrepreneur, and Mike Gascoyne. We had hoped that Petronas would sponsor us but they opted for Sauber instead – a shame that the Malaysian oil and gas company wouldn't get behind a local team. However, Proton, the Malaysian car manufacturer – whose parent company is DRB-HICOM – did grant us permission to use the historic Lotus Racing brand for our team. The team presented our case in late July 2009 and we waited.

A month later, at about midnight, I was in my house in Chester Square, London, and the phone rang. It was Max Mosley.

'You've got a Formula One team.'

I'm not sure I ever quite believed it. From the first call from Déj, to the sums of money involved, to the circus that surrounds the sport: it had all been so surreal.

Now we had to move at breakneck speed. If we wanted to race as Lotus then we had to get a team together, find the drivers and have a car ready inside six months – the pace of events was making *me* tired, let alone the people doing a lot of the work. At the point at which we got the slot, the 'team' consisted of four people: me, Mike, chief operating officer Keith Saunt and general manager Paul Craig. Sylvie, Mike's partner, volunteered to go on to reception and became HR, PR and Marketing.

As 2009 progressed, we contracted two experienced drivers in Jarno Trulli and Heikki Kovalainen for the 2010 season. It was looking good; expensive, but good.

One afternoon in October 2009 I was at home in Kuala Lumpur when my phone rang. I looked at the number and recognized the team centre at Hingham in Norfolk. I picked up and all I could hear was the roar of the team testing our car's engine. That marked the moment when things started to get real.

The unveiling came fast. On 12 February 2010 we gathered the press to present our Lotus Cosworth T127 to the racing world in London's Royal Horticultural Halls. The Halls are spectacular – a glass roof allows sunlight to shine on to the light wooden floors and bounce off the brilliant white walls. The car, painted in the traditional Lotus green and yellow, looked amazing, sitting in front of us on a ramp before the world's press. When I stood up to make a short speech, alongside Clive

Chapman, Stirling Moss, Mike and the drivers, I was still pinching myself:

'I am extremely proud to be here today and to be able to show the world the fruits of the team's hard work over the last five months. We've achieved two major milestones – confirming our entry and unveiling our car – but now the real work starts. Next we move on to testing and the season ahead and I'm confident that the team will exceed expectations wherever we go, and will do so on a wave of support around the world that has been growing daily since we first unleashed Lotus Racing back in September '09.'

Despite a frantic year of headaches and the biggest cash drain I can remember, stepping out on to the starting grid in Bahrain with the Lotus Racing team was a moment I'll never forget. We were proud to be bringing the Lotus brand back to Formula One – it had been absent since 1994. Both drivers finished the race, which was achievement enough. To produce a car on that time scale that made it through a whole Grand Prix was a success.

Most of the things in my life that I love are noisy – live music, aeroplanes, football matches – but few get anywhere close to the decibel level when you're in a Formula One pit lane: the ground shudders with the power and noise of the engines; there's the fumes, the mechanics swarming around, an armoury of tools and tyres; and whenever there's a lull in the engine cacophony, the background buzzes with the fans. It's an attack on every sense – overwhelming and exhausting. In a TV interview after the Bahrain Grand Prix I looked elated but absolutely wrung out, my eyes shining in that bewildered way that you get when you have been through the most intense experience.

The season threw up some incredible highs. Walking on to the starting grid in Malaysia a month later was surreal. I'd felt pretty emotional when the first Grand Prix was put on there in 1999, but to be a team owner in my home town was something for which I really have no words. If I hadn't taken the chance, if I'd hung up on Déj thinking the idea was ridiculous, I'd never have watched my own F1 team compete in Malaysia. Take your chances, I remind myself.

As the season unfolded, it wasn't catastrophic, but neither was it great. We didn't register a point but we did pull off a massive publicity stunt. I was having dinner with Nico Rosberg after the Monaco Grand Prix when Richard Branson walked over with his Virgin Racing CEO Alex Tai. They sat down and we had some banter about our doomed rivalry in the F1 season. Virgin had a team, and like us they weren't doing well. We saw a chance to make the season interesting, so we came up with The Bet. It was simple. The owner of whichever team finished lower in the championship would have to dress up and work as (female) cabin crew on a flight of the winner's airline. That really did liven things up. The prospect of putting on the Virgin uniform made me bring extra pressure to bear on the team for the rest of the season.

When we got to the last race, in Abu Dhabi, we were pretty much neck and neck. Lotus edged it because Heikki had finished twelfth in Japan, which nudged us above Virgin. But it was close – had one of the Virgin drivers taken a higher spot than twelfth in Abu Dhabi I'd be wearing the Virgin cabin crew skirt and blouse.

As it was, Richard would be wearing the red of AirAsia.

I'd taken the uniform with me to the race and when Richard walked past me in the pit, I shoved it into his hands and pinned an AirAsia badge on his shirt. Branson branded. I laughed and, to his credit, he did too.

'See you on board!'

We had three false starts where he had to postpone. All of them reasonable excuses: he needed an operation on his leg because of a skiing accident; then he was invited to the royal wedding of Prince William and Kate Middleton; and finally, when it all looked set, one tragic night, his house on Necker Island burned down. Like I say, he couldn't be blamed for any of that.

Finally, in Perth, Australia, on 13 May 2013, our diaries coincided. We arrived the day before the flight on which Richard was to crew because we were going to a Starlight Children's Foundation fundraiser before the stunt kicked off the next morning. The charity does fantastic work for children who are hospitalized or seriously ill and their families and we announced that AirAsia X would donate $100 AUD for each ticket sold.

Beer in one hand and razor in the other, I beamed first at the audience and then at Richard, and said, 'Now take your trousers off, Branson.'

The whole place erupted as Richard reluctantly stripped down to his boxer shorts and allowed my crew to shave his legs. We went off to continue the party while Richard went back to the hotel to prepare for his five-and-a-half-hour stint of cabin crew work experience. I've never been quite so pleased to have won a bet in my life. So much so that I partied all night, and met Richard leaving the hotel at 4.00 a.m. as I was coming back. I got him to hang on while I showered and changed, and we went to the airport together where my day got just a little bit better as my crew added false eyelashes, rouge and a hefty slap of lipstick to his face.

Richard then went and changed into the AirAsia X uniform. The uniform is a bright-red skirt and blazer, with a white blouse. He went the extra mile and produced a pair of red high-heels to match. We did a brief press conference, he planted a lipstick kiss on my cheek and I picked him up, draping him across my arms horizontally in the way that he would do with his own female cabin crew. The hangover was bad enough but to have to lift his weight was pushing my limits.

When it came to the in-flight safety demonstration, Richard was a shambles. For someone who flies so much, he didn't have a clue about the seat buckle, couldn't get the life vest over his tied-back hair and held the oxygen mask upside down. I was having a ball.

To be fair, Richard threw himself into the role, walking the aisles serving drinks, flirting with passengers and making announcements. Then he decided to get a little bit of his own back by approaching me with a tray stacked with glasses of juice. Egged on by the passengers, he shouted, 'Will I or won't I?'

I pretend begged him not to before he upended the tray into my lap. Changing my clothes was a small price to pay; besides, I'd had a T-shirt printed that read 'Coffee, tea or him' printed on the front and 'Richard served me T&CO' on the back (T&CO is my in-flight coffee brand).

At the press conference in Kuala Lumpur, I summarily sacked him and said, 'He is an entrepreneur, visionary, knight and adventurer; Sir Richard can now also add AirAsia flight attendant to his long list of credentials,' before we ended the whole stunt in true F1 style with a champagne shake-up which we sprayed at each other.

People still remember it. In 2017, I was waiting for a lift in the Beverly Wilshire hotel, Los Angeles. A guy came up to me and asked, 'Are you Tony Fernandes?'

I said I was.

'Won any bets with Richard Branson recently?'

Both Richard and I have been damn good at building brands. That one stunt was worth billions in PR and it came from Formula One. It came from grabbing an opportunity that at first looked like it was just a drain on funds but, with the connections and possibilities it opened up, it's perhaps done more for the AirAsia brand than nearly anything else; and, in relative terms, it cost nothing.

There were many good spin-offs from the whole F1 adventure. And it goes to prove the unbelievable power of networking. Just chance encounters with people can lead to such interesting things. It's like I say about the airline business: why rely on ten heads (on the company board) when you can use the brainpower of 20,000 employees? Or as I say to the cabin crew: why rely on surveys when you can ask 250 million passengers directly? Networking and communicating are essential to drive innovation and development. Our success has been through effective branding but also through the power of networking and my ability to meet and get along with people. I always push myself to establish a rapport with as many people as I can – it's too easy to look inwards and focus exclusively on your own business, but relationships and friendships with people outside your industry will always bring unexpected openings.

At the end of our first F1 season, we had to have a rethink. Although we'd beaten Virgin, we nonetheless hadn't won any points. The biggest mistake we made was probably trying to start the team from scratch, and the promise of a lower-cost Grand Prix never really materialized. Max Mosley's estimate of $40 million was under-powered – I reckon it cost more like $80 million per year to run the team – and that's without building the car. Money was a big issue.

And then we hit a whole wall of problems with the Lotus brand. Our licence to use Lotus Racing was challenged in the courts. The dispute went all the way to the British High Court – I was on the stand for twelve hours on one occasion. At the heart of the conflict was who had the right to licence the Lotus brand name. The Chapman family – the son and widow of Lotus's founder Colin Chapman – were involved, as were David Hunt and Proton, who had originally granted us the licence.

The problem started with David Hunt disputing that we could use the Lotus licence that Proton had granted us. He claimed he owned the Team Lotus brand, while Proton owned Group Lotus, which made Lotus sports cars. The dispute ran through many twists and turns over the course of two years before it was finally resolved – and we knew we'd have to find a new team name.

In the meantime, a knock at the door – and it really was someone knocking on my door because I was in my pyjamas at the time – opened up a new opportunity. When I answered, two men asked me if I wanted to buy Caterham Cars. It's an iconic English sports car brand that still makes high-quality cars. Din and I bought the company in early 2011; as well as believing in the business, we realized it offered us a way out of the Lotus branding dispute. Ironically, Caterham also happens to have a strong connection to Lotus – in the 1970s Colin Chapman, the founder of Lotus, sold Caterham the licence to make one of his most famous cars, 'The Seven' (in fact, that car still has a global reputation and we have forward orders that will take us over a year to fulfil).

In November 2011 we agreed with Proton that we would rebrand our team as Caterham F1, while they would use Lotus F1. We were proud to have brought a much-loved brand back to Formula One and could now press on with Caterham. The legal issues weren't over yet, though – when we tried to use green as our team colours, Lotus claimed we were trying to pass ourselves off as them. But we persevered through the 2011 season and were more consistent on the circuit. Though we still didn't register any points, we finished tenth, which at least gave us a share of the pay-out from Formula One. We had proved that we could compete at the top level.

Progress was so tough to make. When we got to the end of the third season, we were in exactly the same spot and I felt the development of the car itself had actually gone backwards. The next season we finished eleventh and completely out of the money. That was the final straw for me.

In the end, the Formula One venture was just too exhausting to pursue any further. We sold Caterham F1 (but not Caterham Cars) in 2014. The issues continued for the new owners and just four months later they dissolved the team. A great shame.

Despite all that, I still think that one day we'll be back on the starting grid. When I tell people this, they laugh and think I'm mad. That just reminds me of the reaction when I first said I was starting an airline – it makes me want to do it all the more. As a sport, now that Bernie Ecclestone has sold up and moved on, Formula One is going through some fundamental changes. I think those changes are long overdue because the racing just hasn't been as exciting as it should be for years.

In football – for all its sins – you never know who is going to win. No one in their right mind would have put money on Leicester to take the Premier League title in the 2015–16 season. But in Formula One, Caterham would never win a race. The sport has become too much of a procession, with the teams with the deepest pockets pretty much guaranteed to share the podium places between them. It's also become too technical; the engineers are the most important factor, whereas I think it should all be about the skill of the drivers. If you look at the greatest sports stars of the past, Bjorn Borg didn't win all those titles because his racket was better than Ilie Năstase's racket or because his team were bigger than Jimmy Connors' team; he did it because he was superior, player versus player. The same applies in cricket: Viv Richards and Sunil Gavaskar weren't brilliant batsmen because of the bat they used, it was because their timing, eye and stroke play were second to none.

Throughout my life, I've tried to make things simpler,

and that's what they should do in F1. The cars are so complex, and the rules ridiculously so, it obscures the competition between the drivers, which is what racing fans go to see. Not so long ago, Eddie Jordan started a team and won a Grand Prix but that would never happen now. So there should be much more emphasis on the actual racing, and the cars should be far more standardized.

The complexity and the money involved is also restricting the sport's appeal. My sense is that the number of young people watching is going down, which doesn't bode well for its future popularity. My sense also is that it isn't as global as it should be. Only four of the twenty-four current (2017) starting-grid drivers are non-European, and none are from the Far East or South East Asia. The likelihood of there being a Chinese or Malaysian winner is non-existent. Some of that has to do with the money involved if you want to become a driver. How does a poor kid from Vietnam or India get to be an F1 driver when it costs millions of dollars to get there?

Still, so much came from the F1 experience. Not only did we give the AirAsia brand the global prominence I felt it deserved, it opened up doors for me personally and also for our companies. Without F1, I wouldn't be involved at QPR, and we also acquired two pretty exciting companies along the way.

Caterham Cars hasn't really been touched as a company since the seventies, so there is so much potential to expand through the use of new technologies – I feel a bit like I did at the birth of AirAsia. I've owned a Smart car for years and have always felt they are the future, so at Caterham I want to develop electric cars and get them to a wider audience. I also believe that we'll start to produce 3D-printed cars. By developing these technologies we'll be able to take car manufacturing to a much greener, more sustainable place that fits with my beliefs. I wouldn't be surprised if we built something really special at Caterham in the coming years.

Mirus, the other company we have set up, is a lightweight aeroplane-seat manufacturer. It uses the principles learned in constructing Formula One seats to create aircraft seats that are greener and lighter than any currently on the market. Reducing the weight of a single seat, even by a fraction, brings huge efficiencies in fuel usage on all flights. I think there's great potential here too.

Formula One was a blast. I don't regret it for a second. I learned so much about best practice and technology, much of which has been fed back into AirAsia. And then there was the global exposure for AirAsia – the association with the circuit and some of the most famous brands in the world rubbed off on us. You can't go from having two planes to 200 without stepping up your brand building: sponsoring Man United and F1 cars are part and parcel of that.

I personally gained a lot of confidence from Formula One. Suddenly I wasn't a little Asian businessman tinkering around with a low-cost airline, I was actually on the global stage, a team principal of Lotus Racing, and appearing every other week at some of the biggest sporting events in the world. It's important because people then look at you and treat you differently. Petronas once told me that our cost of borrowing was lower because of F1 – it gave us a recognizable, valuable name.

I met a lot of top people in the F1 world. Bernie

Ecclestone is an incredible guy: he gets good and bad press but to me he is brilliant. His advice to me was always to grab opportunities whenever I saw them. Ron Dennis is a powerhouse too. I learned so much from him – the determination, energy and precision he brings to his work is inspiring.

Then there's the flamboyant Italian businessman Flavio Briatore. Flavio had been involved with the Benetton team which became Renault. His past was a bit chequered, like the Grand Prix finishing flag, but without Formula One I'd have never met him. He and Bernie Ecclestone at that time owned the majority stake in Queens Park Rangers, the west London football club. He called me one day in late 2010.

'Hi, Tony, it's Flavio. I'm sitting here with Bernie. Do you want to buy 30 per cent of QPR?'

10. We Are QPR

Soundtrack: 'Papa's Got a Brand New Pigbag' by Pigbag

On the pitch at Wembley, celebrating our epic win in the final, the world-famous midfielder lifted me on to his shoulders. Around us, more than 40,000 fans chanted and sang our names.

No, it wasn't a dream. Below me I could hear Joey Barton groan.

'Jesus, Tony, could you lose some weight?'

He looked back, grinned at me and carried on chanting.

'WE ARE QPR

SAID WE ARE QPR

WE ARE QPR . . .'

It was 5.15 on a sunny May afternoon in 2014. Apart from being a bit concerned about Joey Barton's back, this was probably (birth of children aside) the happiest moment of my life: we'd just been promoted back to the Premier League after a season in the Championship. To win a final at Wembley is any football fan's dream; as a club owner, it was unreal.

Football has brought me some of the most memorable days. Watching Brazil on television with my dad in the seventies; the first time I saw West Ham play on TV; getting my West Ham jersey at Selfridges with my mum; going to my first game; and then finding myself in my forties travelling on the team bus to the Etihad Stadium for a championship and relegation decider, and that afternoon at Wembley: highs you don't come down from very fast.

While I was setting up AirAsia and dealing with all the problems that were being thrown our way, I still managed to get to a few West Ham games and became friendly with some of the former players who were involved with the club.

In late 2006, the West Ham legend Tony Cottee and a couple of other people approached me to ask whether I wanted to buy West Ham. The club was eventually sold to the Icelandic pair of Björgólfur Guðmundsson and Eggert Magnússon but that approach planted a seed in my mind. I carried on going to Upton Park, keeping in touch with the key players there.

When the Icelandic financial crisis hit in 2007–8, the owners went bust and the opportunity to buy the club came up again. We started talking to the administrators and were getting close to a deal. As things progressed, Din was called back to Kuala Lumpur but I stayed. Within a few days, I rang Din and told him to get over to London to sign. Just as he landed, the administrators called to say that they'd sold the club to David Sullivan and David Gold. We knew they were in the race but thought we were going to get our noses over the line first. Disappointed, we both flew back to Kuala Lumpur. As it was, we were just getting into Formula One and the financial pressures were pretty intense.

Flavio Briatore famously said of his involvement in football, 'I will never invest in a football club again – it's only ever a good idea if you're very rich and looking for ways to waste your money. In two years, you'll be very poor and won't have that problem any more.'

Then again, I find it difficult to say 'no' when I'm offered something I care so much about. A couple of years after the close call with West Ham, I got that contact from Flavio. He and Bernie Ecclestone had picked me as a candidate to buy Flavio's share because they thought I had lots of energy and could help turn things round. He'd been there for about four years and had had a pretty rough time. The fans hadn't responded well to a number of things, including a redesign of the club's crest and a hike in season ticket prices, despite the wealth of the owners. Changing the mascot from Jude the Black Cat to a tiger was the final straw (black cats are unlucky in Italy but Jude had been around for ever). And Flavio had had problems off the pitch after a series of scandals in F1 which put him in trouble with the FA, who were questioning whether he was a 'fit and proper person' to own a club. It was messy but I was interested. Before I knew it, Bernie Ecclestone said he'd run his course there and I could buy his share too. Once again, I was being offered something and, once again, I thought to myself, 'If not now, then when?' The outcome was never really in doubt.

Before I bought it (and I was really keen, what with my QPR history and love of football), I went to the first pre-season friendly with Flavio and met Neil Warnock, the experienced manager, and a few of the players – who didn't know who the hell I was. We negotiated throughout the summer until the first game of the season, their first game back in the Premiership after fifteen years in the Championship.

We were at home to Bolton – who always seem to play a significant role in my QPR life – and we lost 4–0. An unhappy start to the season and a cold shower on the optimism we'd felt over the summer. I was sitting with Flavio and the board in the directors' box. About fifteen minutes before the end, with no hope of getting back into the game, most of the others left, leaving me sitting on my own. On *Match of the Day* that night the camera panned over us all sitting there at the start of the game, all smiles and laughter; and then they cruelly showed another sequence of me sitting alone in the box, hand on chin, looking glumly at the pitch. 'Welcome to the Premiership,' I thought.

Despite the result, we signed the deal. Owning a football club felt as surreal as the Formula One experience – another sticker fantasy from my tuck box fulfilled. Amit Bhatia and Ruben Gnanalingam remained involved, while Din and I took over Bernie and Flavio's shares. The ride of my sporting life began when I walked from the boardroom with a QPR shirt in my hand.

From that day, 18 August 2011, to the appointment of Ian Holloway as manager in November 2016, there hasn't been a moment to draw breath. Only now do I feel we have some proper control. From really not knowing anything about running a club, I now feel that we are in the most secure situation we have been since 2011 (and possibly, with respect to Flavio and Bernie, a while before then too). It's taken a long time, and a lot of effort, pain and money, but we're now at the stage I'd like to have been at the season after I took over: we have a culture that encourages growth from within; players who are passionate about playing for the club and who respect the fans and the crest week in week out; the right people in place to do the right jobs; and a sense of where we want to go and how we're going to get there. As always in football, it's not perfect and the trajectory won't be smooth, but we have the right elements to succeed.

Back in August 2011, things were not so clear. Every game brought a deluge of tension, anxiety which sometimes ended in real joy but more often ended in despair. Football is the most passionate sport and true fans veer from one extreme of emotion to the other – often in every minute of every game. As chairman, you feel each of these and then you add the stress of being responsible for the funding, the security and the direction of the club. It's a huge weight to carry.

Neil Warnock had done an amazing job in the previous season, getting us promoted from the Championship, and we hoped he would be able to build on that momentum when we started in the top tier of English football. As a new chairman facing your first season in charge in the toughest league in the world, it was a baptism of fire.

The second game, we went up to Everton and we won 1–0. After the previous week's loss, this felt more like it. I was listening to the game on the radio and it brought back memories of Paddy Feeny and my shortwave radio. This time, though, the fans were singing my name in the background, which was a proud moment.

And then we lost to Wigan away. It was still only August – thirty-five matches to go. We focused on improving the squad and made some significant signings: Joey Barton on a free transfer from Newcastle; Shaun Wright-Phillips for £4 million from Man City; Luke Young from Aston Villa; Anton Ferdinand from Sunderland; and Armand Traoré from Arsenal. It was a pretty good crop of professionals to bring into the club but progress throughout the autumn was uneven – if it could be called progress at all. We drew at home to Newcastle, beat Wolves away and then got hammered 6–0 by Fulham at Craven Cottage.

By early in 2012 it was pretty clear that we were in big trouble: we'd got only seventeen points from twenty games. After a home defeat to Norwich on 2 January we went to MK Dons in the Third Round of the FA Cup on 7 January and drew. Everyone knew it wasn't good enough.

The pressure was on from the fans and the board and I was faced with my first really big decision as chairman: should I let Neil Warnock go? I agonized over it. Neil is a special guy, he knows how to get the best out of players and he knows the Championship inside out; I liked and respected him. But the feeling on the board was that he had lost the dressing room and so I felt it was right for the club to get someone new in.

At the time our CEO was a guy I'd hired called Philip Beard. I knew Andy Anson, who was commercial director at Man United, through AirAsia's sponsorship deal with the club and I'd asked him whether he'd take the job when I first bought QPR. Andy declined because the time wasn't right for him, but he recommended Phil, who was running the O2 Arena in east London. Although he had never run a football club, Phil's commercial, legal and personal credentials were impeccable. My reasoning was that coming from outside had been a plus for me at AirAsia so I went with Andy's recommendation.

So, I told Phil to sack Neil. In the meantime, agents had been calling offering various managers to replace Neil even as we were discussing letting him go. Within twelve hours of him going, Kia Joorabchian, a well-known figure in football and the man, amongst other things, at the centre of the controversy surrounding the 'ownership' of Carlos Tevez and Javier Mascherano, called about Mark Hughes, the former Man United and Chelsea striker. Mark had made the transition to management successfully at Blackburn and then, under huge pressure, at Man City. After Sheikh Mansour had let him go from City, he'd moved to be one of QPR's closest neighbours at Fulham but had resigned after just over ten months because he felt that the club didn't have ambition.

I met him at my house in London. On paper, Mark's credentials were strong: his record at Fulham and Blackburn was solid. I questioned him at length about his stint at Man City and he was adamant that given time he'd have achieved more, but the new owners had been in a rush for trophies. I asked him what he'd do with QPR and he talked a lot about pre-match preparations, about studying the opposition; he came across as highly organized, methodical and analytical. Added to that, of course, he'd played at the highest level for Barcelona, Man United and Chelsea, so he knew the game inside and out as both a player and manager.

We announced Neil's departure, and Neil in his professional and gracious way released a statement that touched me:

Obviously, I'm very disappointed but, having achieved so much, I leave the club with a great sense of pride. I have enjoyed my time here more than anywhere else and the

QPR fans have been brilliant with me – they deserve success. My biggest regret is that the takeover didn't happen earlier, because that would have given me the opportunity to bring in the targets I'd pinpointed all last summer and probably given us a better chance to succeed in the Premier League. The board at QPR are hugely ambitious and I wish them every success for the future. I've been involved in the game a long time and I will be spending the immediate future with my family and friends before deciding my next career move.

On 10 January 2012, we proudly announced that we had secured Mark Hughes's services. I was pleased that we'd got through the process so quickly and felt we'd made a good choice. The next thing I knew, I was being whacked on Twitter with abuse from angry fans, accusing me of hiring a Man City reject, of spouting 'shit' the whole time, of trying to sell the best players to make a fast buck. I was even denounced for my atrocious spelling. That's something you don't get running an airline! I responded as best I could, urging the fans to remain positive and taking criticisms on the chin.

Mark came in and we spent quite a bit of money in the January transfer window, adding Nedum Onuoha (£4.2 million) from Man City, Djibril Cissé (£4.4 million) from Lazio and Bobby Zamora (£5 million) from Fulham. In QPR terms, that was a big investment.

But our poor form continued. Easter approached and it looked like we were really going down. In March 2012, I was in Japan. We were playing Liverpool at Loftus Road. I have an internal body clock which wakes me up whenever we're playing. So it was 2.00 a.m. or something in Japan when the match kicked off. At that stage of the season, we were level on points with Wigan but one point behind Bolton, who also had a game in hand. Wolves were bottom but only three points behind us. It was tight and things were looking bad. We went one down and then with twenty minutes to go Dirk Kuyt scored a second for Liverpool. Ruben texted, 'We're dead, we're down. We'll just rebuild and come back.'

I texted back, 'No, don't give up. We could just turn it around.'

And then Shaun Derry got one back for us, followed by Cissé, who equalized with four minutes to go, and then Jamie Mackie finished it off in injury time. A stunning comeback. Unbelievable. One of the greatest QPR games I've witnessed.

I really thought that we'd turned it around but then we went to Sunderland and got well beaten, so things looked gloomy again. Then Adel Taarabt stepped up – he'd had an incredible last season in the Championship but he had been inconsistent in the Premiership, until he suddenly started dominating games. We went on a bit of a run, beating Arsenal, Swansea and Spurs – games that we had no right to win. We also had some pretty bad results – losing 6–1 to our hated rivals Chelsea was particularly painful – so it was touch and go.

The last home game of the season arrived. The situation was on a knife edge. Wolves were already down but Blackburn, Bolton and us were fighting it out to avoid the remaining two relegation spots. Blackburn were three points behind us and Bolton. We each had thirty-four points; our consolation was that our goal difference was better than Bolton's but we had two very tough games. The first was this home fixture against Stoke and then away at Man City, who were gunning for the title at the other end of the league. Meanwhile, Bolton were at home to West Brom – a game that was winnable – and then away at Stoke; again, a game they could possibly walk away from with three points. Blackburn were due to play Wigan on Monday night and then were away at Chelsea for the final game of the season. I was less concerned about them. The struggle between us and Bolton was what worried me.

That Sunday was one of the most stressful days I can remember. I tried to focus hard on what was going on on the pitch but was desperate for news of Bolton at West Brom. You could feel the tension around Loftus Road, anxious QPR fans monitoring their phones constantly as the game played out in front of us. After twenty-four minutes a huge sigh went round the ground: Bolton had gone one up through a penalty. Half-time came and we were at 0–0, Bolton were winning and would be two points clear of us if the results stayed that way. Worse news followed. Bolton went two up thanks to a West Brom own goal. My reaction to the goal was a fan's reaction, not an owner's – I choked back the tears and tried to focus on giving the team as much support as possible. After all, one goal would put us in the same position as Bolton.

Then things changed. Three minutes after Billy Jones's own goal, Chris Brunt pulled one back for West Brom. It was 2–1 to Bolton. With five minutes to go, we were still at 0–0 and my positive energy was ebbing away. Then in the eighty-ninth minute Anton Ferdinand headed to Cissé, who poked it in. We all went bananas. At the very least we'd matched Bolton's win. Then the celebrations got wilder as we heard that West Brom had equalized.

That night in Shepherd's Bush was some night. The directors and staff went out on the town, ending up at a pub called the Defectors Weld on Shepherd's Bush Green, which is about a ten-minute walk from the flat I used to rent on the Uxbridge Road. When I woke up the following morning, the reality hit me hard. Although we were two points clear of Bolton we weren't actually safe from relegation. In fact, we were anything but safe given that we still had to go play Manchester City at the Etihad Stadium and pray that Bolton lost to Stoke. In a twist that only football can deliver, Man City had to beat us to win the title. Everything rested on these two results.

These are the kinds of days you live for. The excitement, stress, intensity are life-defining. I'll never forget the scale of the day and how I felt at the end of it. And football is a game where there's no in-between emotion; it's either ecstasy or you're suicidal.

And so a week later, 13 May 2012, Din and I flew into Manchester overnight from Kuala Lumpur. I didn't sleep all night. We went to a hotel and then met the players, who were having their pre-match briefings. If we won – highly unlikely – we stayed up; but if Bolton lost, whatever happened, we were safe. The day unfolded in a way that would test the strongest heart. Stoke went one up against Bolton after twelve minutes and we all cheered. But then in the thirty-ninth minute we suffered double agony: City scored against us and Bolton got one back at Stoke. On the stroke of half-time, Bolton got a second and we went into the dressing room knowing that if the results stayed that way we'd be down. Amit, Ruben, Din and I were all super-depressed. All the Man City directors were consoling – 'Don't worry, you'll be back next season.'

Three minutes into the second half, the unbelievable happened: Cissé scored an equalizer. The drama really started. Joey Barton was sent off for a foul on Carlos Tevez after fifty-five minutes, but with about twenty-five minutes left, Jamie Mackie popped up and buried a header to give us the lead. I turned to look at the others and we went crazy. If we could go crazier, we did, when Jonathan Walters equalized for Stoke. As things stood, we were staying up and handing the title to Manchester United. The Etihad was a cauldron. City fans couldn't believe they'd be robbed of the title on the last day of the season by QPR, while we were going berserk at the prospect of survival.

The rest of the directors' box was silent and immobile. We didn't care. Five minutes to go, we were still 2–1 up. Two minutes to go, then Džeko scored for them and Agüero finished it off.

It didn't matter because Stoke held on and Bolton were relegated. The City fans were delirious and we were beside ourselves. It was that rare situation when everyone in the ground was ecstatic. City had won the title for the first time in forty-four years and finally felt they could start to look United fans in the eye again. We had got through our toughest test and I had been part of one of the most ridiculous games I've ever seen. Punch-drunk, we got on the plane with the team back to London. There was a lot of celebrating but I also picked up that Joey Barton was a bit ostracized by the rest of the team because of the sending-off.

The feeling inside the club was that we could build on this, using the momentum from our amazing escape.

Reflecting on that first season, I realized that the mistake I made was letting emotion get the better of me and trusting people too much. When you come to a new business and one that is as high profile as Premier League football, you presume that everyone knows what they're doing, but that's not always true; just because people have been in their jobs for a long time, it doesn't mean they know what they're doing. It was similar to the time in Warner where we bought the RAP label and their fantastic artists – talent doesn't necessarily translate into performance, talent has to be managed. In music, it's slightly less obvious than in football, because playing football is all about character. If you've got the right character, you'll perform to the best of your ability; if your character isn't up to it, you won't. Even after my experience with RAP, I went against my instincts and let things happen without questioning enough. Then there was the problem of distance. I was still based in Kuala Lumpur, running AirAsia from there and jetting all over the place with the Formula One team, so I simply could not be at QPR enough. And, because I wasn't there every day, I didn't see things through my own eyes.

It brought home to me strongly how important physical presence and visibility are for a leader. They are important not just to keep the staff focused and to make sure that the culture of openness grows but also so that you can gauge the mood, see the day-to-day interactions and hear the snippets that are telling.

So I missed seeing what was happening on the training

183

ground and whether such-and-such a player was really putting a proper shift in – either in training, around the club or on the pitch. If I'd been more aware of that I think I'd have realized quicker that often the salaries being paid were far bigger than the effort I saw on the pitch. It was naivety really. I came from the standpoint that if you're being paid so much money, you work your butt off; but some of these players simply didn't.

Over the summer of 2012, we thought we'd bought well: a lot of players came in on free transfers, like José Bosingwa from Chelsea, but they also demanded mega salaries because they were at the end of their careers. Ji-sung Park was a huge signing for me in particular because he's an Asian player and over there he's a god. Unfortunately, he was half the player he had been. And it turns out that when we looked at the analysis, he hadn't played that many full games – he'd been used more as a super-sub. Then we got Cissé on a permanent deal but he wasn't as good in the second season. We always felt we needed two centre backs but people were asking stupid money because they knew we were pushovers. I put a stop to that.

Mark sent Joey Barton off to Marseille on loan which I fought hard against but lost. Joey has been a big part of my football life. Joey is direct, like me, and can put people's backs up (again like me), but he tells it as he sees it and, in football, that's worth something.

When he was at QPR, he said to me many times that we were going down the wrong track and signing the wrong players. His point was that signing old professionals wasn't good for the club but he could never quite establish himself enough with the managers to convince them. He was kind of involved in Neil Warnock's dismissal but then he and Mark Hughes couldn't see eye to eye on anything. When Mark sent him off on loan, we really missed the backbone, his leadership and his fighting spirit on and off the pitch. He's a smart guy who just had a loose fuse. If Joey didn't see people playing 100 per cent or the way he felt they should be playing, he went after them, so he caused friction in the camp. After he had his baby he calmed down a bit and I think if he had stayed with us things might have gone better. I pushed hard with Mark to keep him but Mark wouldn't budge, saying that the club would be better without him. I even tried to get him back at the beginning of the 2016–17 season but we couldn't afford him and he went to Burnley.

It's one of the bad sides of football: if people don't like you, they cut you out. Whereas I'd always try to look for other options and work things through, there's a ruthlessness about football that can be counterproductive.

Joey predicted that QPR wouldn't win a game for two months in the 2012–13 season. He was wrong; it was more like four. In hindsight, this was the worst season we had and set us back a long way. We lost the spine of the team and bought in too many players.

We played well at the beginning despite having a nightmare first game against Swansea which we lost 5–0. In an emotional overreaction, I signed Júlio César from Inter Milan, which was a disaster because we should have stood by Rob. Over the course of the next few months we didn't play badly but only picked up three points from nine games. You can't recover from that kind of start. Some players who'd done well the previous season just didn't perform – Taarabt, for example, whom we'd made permanent on a big contract – and I just don't think the team were right mentally. The dressing room was divided and factional, and the team lacked motivation. It was probably the first time I really understood that you could be paying someone a lot of money but they weren't always going to pay you back by playing 100 per cent.

We sacked Mark Hughes, which didn't surprise anyone given our results. By the time he'd gone in November, we had four points from twelve games and we hadn't won a game – not the kind of record to inspire the fans, management or players. Things looked bad but Harry Redknapp came in and we all felt if anyone could save us, it would be Harry. Sadly, not even Harry's relegation-defying talents could change our abysmal start to the season. Three weeks before the end of the season we were relegated after a 0–0 draw at Reading, who were also demoted. We went down with a whimper. Leaving the Premiership turned out to be a good thing although on 28 April 2013 it felt like the end of the world.

Football never relents. The excitement of our first season back in the Championship since I'd become chairman was as great, if not more so, than our tumultuous first season in the Premier League.

Joey Barton came back from Marseille, adding steel to the midfield and to our team mentality, and we started on fire – not losing a game until the end of October. Then came a difficult period over Christmas, and an inconsistent run: we lost seven of the last seventeen games and dropped out of the top two. Leicester and Burnley were steaming ahead at the top but we hung in there and ended up seven points ahead of Wigan in the play-off places. We were tight at the back but couldn't score goals either so most games were close.

We faced Wigan in the two-match play-offs. If we beat them, we'd go to Wembley to face the winner out of Derby and Brighton. Wigan have always been a bogey team for me. There's something about their history with West Ham and QPR that spooks me. The first leg was at the DW Stadium and, as always when I'm nervous, I arrived very early. After an hour or two of solitary pacing, I bumped into Jamie Redknapp, who was on Sky Sports duties; he tried to calm me down. I went to see the players to try to inspire them but I think everyone's nerves were jangling.

The game was tough but we managed a 0–0 draw, which put us in good shape for the return leg at Loftus Road. The day dawned and it was beautiful, temperatures were up and the evening was perfect for football . . . until we went 1–0 down after nine minutes to a James Perch goal. The worst possible start. I had that Wigan feeling again until Joey Barton got the players in a huddle at half-time and something changed. A few weeks earlier, Joey had persuaded Phil Beard, our CEO, to bring in Steve Black, a motivational speaker who had worked with Jonny Wilkinson. Steve's messages had been about keeping a simple focus and it was working. The communications team created a message on the back of that which was simply: 'WE ARE TOGETHER'. That half-time huddle expressed that thought perfectly and it seemed to galvanize the team.

Charlie Austin got one back with a penalty after Junior Hoilett was brought down inside the box. That left about fifteen minutes on the clock. We'd already seen Rob Green make some fantastic saves and then Wigan hit the post. We had been lucky but I still felt it was ours for the taking. The atmosphere was unbelievable at Loftus Road – under the floodlights the crowd didn't let up for a second. Again, a night to remember, the sort that makes football so special. Before extra time, a monsoon started, the rain bucketing down like a bad day in Malaysia, and then Joey got everyone together for another huddle.

I thought we were heading to penalties but in the first half of extra time, Charlie Austin diverted Bobby Zamora's ball in and we all went bananas. Absolute pandemonium in Loftus Road. Wigan came back at us hard and Rob Kiernan nearly equalized with a deflection. You could hear the whole crowd suck in its breath.

When the final whistle eventually came, there was a pitch invasion. The rain was still hammering down, I was leaping up and down like a lunatic, people were singing my name and all the investors were there. By the time we'd celebrated on the pitch, getting soaked and taking selfies with the fans, it was probably midnight, but we opened the champagne in the dressing room and partied long into the night. Dave Whelan, chairman of Wigan, left in his helicopter before the end, which I thought a bit odd, but I guess he's an experienced chairman who's seen it all before. The excitement for us lasted less than twenty-four hours; then we had to focus on the final hurdle to the Premiership.

At last, 24 May 2014 dawned. The day of the play-off final against Derby at Wembley. We got 40,000 QPR flags and then a hundred or so volunteers from the QPR staff, QPR in the Community Trust and fans put a flag on every seat in the QPR end. When the team emerged, the scene was a dream – a churning sea of blue and white flags dominated one end of the ground. To take your team to Wembley is a feeling that so few people have had and one that I wouldn't trade for anything.

We got completely outplayed by Derby; at half-time it was amazing it was still o–o. Things got worse in the second half, when Gary O'Neil brought down Johnny Russell and we were down to ten men. This was about as low as it could get: we were at the end of a long, long season, there were over thirty minutes left and we were still being pummelled. It was like a boxing match going all the rounds with one boxer being permanently pinned to the ropes. I was amazed we were still standing but had a sense that, having hung on so long, we might just come away with something.

I turned to Ruben. 'We're going to win this. Whenever we get a player sent off, we'll win or get a result.'

Phil Beard, sitting next to me, was despondent. 'Let's get it over and done with. We can regroup next season and push again.'

The eighty-ninth minute came and we still hadn't had a single shot. Junior Hoilett, who had done little of note all season, ploughed his way down the wing, crossed and Richard Keogh, Derby's captain, scuffed his clearance. It went straight to Bobby Zamora, who buried it first time. Elation! Ecstasy! I don't think there are the words to describe the feeling. Derby had no time to come back at us.

When the final whistle went, it was unbelievable. No emotion in my fifty-three years can better that. The game was *Roy of the Rovers* stuff – except I don't think even in a comic you could have got away with that ending.

We were presented with the trophy and, well, what more could you want? We went down to the pitch and 40,000 QPR fans were singing my name and all the great QPR chants. Then Joey Barton picked me up; the *Daily Star* had the picture on the back page the next day.

I've relived that moment a thousand times. We had a party at Loftus Road for all the staff and the players. Everyone could bring three or four family or friends so it was a big do which again went into the early hours. I didn't sleep that night, just kept watching the highlights over and over and over. The following day we threw another party at Loftus Road and about 8,000 supporters came along to celebrate with the team. QPR are is such a family club and the fans are so local that the atmosphere felt familiar. Never one to miss an opportunity to showcase other brands, I presented Harry with a Caterham Seven and a personalized number plate to show our appreciation.

We were back in the Premiership but I was nervous about our chances again. We had lots of meetings about budgets and players but we seemed to be repeating the mistakes of 2012–13. Harry Redknapp surprised me a bit by choosing not to use academy players like he had at West Ham. He did the opposite; he wanted to use players he knew and trusted. So he signed Rio Ferdinand, which we argued about. Joey was clear that, much as he respected Rio as a man and a player, he wasn't right for the team.

But we also signed Matt Phillips and Leroy Fer, who were good signings. We got Sandro even though Les

Ferdinand – our director of football – warned us against him. Sandro had been an animal at Spurs but was a major disappointment for us – he just wasn't fit enough. We had a core of some good players – Rob Green was great, for example – but our defence was weak so we let in a lot of goals. They were the best of a not-so-great bunch.

It became clear that rather than going after journeymen from the Premier League we should target players from the lower leagues. They tend to be of better value and hungry. By the end of the 2016–17 season, none of our players were ex-Premiership – everyone had come from lower leagues or the academy. And I felt much better about it. There are only a couple of players who've been there virtually the whole time I've been in charge: Nedum Onuoha and Jamie Mackie (who left for a couple of seasons but came back). The rest have come and gone.

The 2014–15 season was another one to forget on the pitch but behind the scenes it marked the beginning of a sea change. We won only eight games out of thirty-eight and finished bottom – three points behind Burnley and five behind Hull. There were many problems.

Joey really didn't have the support he needed in midfield and the players we brought in just weren't up to it. There were a couple of silver linings, though. Over the summer I got a call from Les Ferdinand, a QPR legend who scored eighty goals in 160 or so appearances for the club. Les just said, 'I really want to do something with QPR.'

So we arranged to meet in Jakarta and got on like a house on fire. I realized that, although he was raw, his heart was in the right place and he could be the person we needed day-to-day at the club who could bring in a bit of discipline. So we signed Les up first as head of football operations to help develop the academy talent. He arrived in October and brought in Chris Ramsey as academy manager; they had worked together at Tottenham so knew each other well. Both Phil Beard and Harry were a bit pissed off about the appointments, I think, because to an extent they diminished their own roles. But it was the start of a new plan.

In February 2015, Harry quit – just after the transfer window closed. Harry needed knee surgery but I also think he just felt he couldn't face another relegation battle; perhaps he felt that, with Les coming in, the focus would be more on youth. I like Harry and we have a lot of time for each other so I don't hold it against him. In fact, in the long term, he did us a favour.

We looked at various replacements and Tim Sherwood was top of the list. He had done a good job at Tottenham before being sacked the year before. Tim and I talked a lot and I liked him but he is highly opinionated and vocal about it. It would have made for a tougher and I think perhaps more combative kind of relationship. As it happened, he decided at the last minute to go to Aston Villa. In the end, we appointed Chris Ramsey in a caretaker role until the end of the season. Chris had been doing a great job at the academy, he knew the players and understood the club, so we thought we'd give him the chance to step up.

At the same time, we expanded Les's role to include player recruitment and that, Phil Beard felt, diminished *his* job too much. Phil had been with us from the beginning but I think we were starting to move in different directions and recognized that we needed someone with more football experience. He resigned in February, a month after Harry.

Within four weeks, we'd lost our CEO and manager: football is never ever not challenging. However, another silver lining appeared in the form of Lee Hoos, who we persuaded to come in as CEO. Lee is probably one of our best signings. He had experience as CEO at Burnley, Leicester, Southampton and Fulham. He knows football through and through and he's made a big difference. With Lee and Les in place, the club feels transformed and Ruben and I feel that it is in safe hands, so we can just watch the budgets. My problem with not being at the club enough is offset by having people there every day whom I trust to get on and do things the way I want them done.

After Chris's first game in charge, we thought we'd got it spot-on: we won away at Sunderland, the first away game we had won all season. Rio Ferdinand and a few others messaged me to say that they thought Chris was OK. Even so, I started talking to Paul Clement – he was Carlo Ancelotti's second-in-command at Real Madrid. I thought he would have been brilliant for the club. But Paul didn't want to leave Real Madrid at least until the end of the season. So we carried on with Chris. He couldn't turn it around and we finished bottom with only thirty points.

Looking back, we never had a pause to build a stable squad. From the second I took over, we were fighting relegation, survived, bought players to stay up but got relegated, fought to get back up and then were fighting to stay up again. There was no stability. And at the end of that season, the average age of the squad was nearly thirty-one – we had a lot of older players on big contracts who weren't putting enough in to justify their wages. It was the wrong way forward – just as Joey had been saying.

Although Chris Ramsey did well, he wasn't quite right for the job and we let him go back to managing the youth squad at the beginning of November. Neil Warnock helped us out for a month while we hunted down our next manager. I actually wanted Neil to stay on – we got some good results under him and it was impressive to see what he achieved in such a short space of time. But the longer view prevailed: we needed someone younger who could rebuild the side.

We hired Jimmy Floyd Hasselbaink, Chelsea's former striker and twice winner of the Premier League Golden Boot. Since retiring, Jimmy had been working at his managerial career and had been successful. When we got him in, he'd secured promotion for Burton Albion from League One to the Championship – the first time the club had reached that level of competition. We thought Jimmy had everything: he was young, strong and a striker so we assumed he'd want to play attacking football. In fact, we played ugly football and looked like a struggling side under Jimmy.

As the 2015–16 season progressed, Jimmy couldn't make his mark on the club and our results were poor. We ended up a mediocre twelfth but hoped that the summer and the new season would start better.

I was, in the end, the person to say that we had to let Jimmy go because I was so frustrated by the way we were playing. We ended up drawing more games than we won or lost and the side to me felt like it lacked ambition. Jimmy had some strange ideas – playing without a striker sometimes – and I thought we were going to struggle because he was obsessed with one player, Tjaronn Chery, whom he built the team around, and wasn't giving other players like Conor Washington a chance. So eventually we decided we should let him go after we lost to Brentford 2–0. Les did the deed on 5 November 2016 and I went home to Kuala Lumpur.

Results on the pitch were the problem during Jimmy's spell as the manager, but to give him his due, he – along with Chris Ramsey – had started cleaning up the club. He did a great job of moving the older players on, changing the culture and taking the academy more seriously. Finally our development programmes were getting the focus they deserved. One statistic shows the effect of their work: at the start of the 2016–17 season, the average age of the first team squad was down to around twenty-four.

Less tangibly but just as importantly, the culture was starting to become more like AirAsia – where players come through the ranks and find their best position. Up to that point, I don't think QPR had had a player come up through the academy to the first team. Now we've got five or six players who've all 'graduated' and are either on the bench in the squad or in the team.

After we let Jimmy go, we looked at all kinds of managers. Then our head of communications, Ian Taylor, who's a sounding board for me, said: 'Why don't you try Ian Holloway?' On the other hand, Lee Hoos, our new CEO, and Les Ferdinand, director of football, were a bit unsure. Their view was that although he was a former player and probably one of the most energetic managers around, Holly might not be strategic enough to move the club in the direction we all agreed was needed. We wanted a new manager to develop the academy and to have a more organic approach to the way the whole club functioned, training players through the academy into the first team.

I just called Ian up and we started to talk. I was blown away. Here was a manager who loved the club so much he didn't even ask about the salary! Ian's focus was on the job alone and doing the best for QPR. His attitude rose above even the most dedicated people I'd met.

I spoke to Ruben and said, 'This guy's unreal; he's not interested in money or the deal, he just wants to be QPR manager.'

I felt it was the right fit for the club. So I pushed for him and we got him.

Holly's first game was at home against Norwich. Norwich got a player sent off in the second minute. We went 2–0 up, Norwich got one back and the last fifteen minutes were really edgy. We held on for 2–1.

The season ended OK. We're finally rebuilding. After five years I feel that we've got what I've always dreamed about: a QPR team that really are a QPR team through and through. Les Ferdinand, Ian Holloway and Marc Bircham, all former QPR players, are now at the heart of running the club.

Holly has been picking academy players – two are now starting for the first team and there are five or six hovering on the fringes. That hadn't happened in my five years as chairman.

Other aspects of the club have started to flourish. We've got a robust scouting system in place after Les Ferdinand brought in Gary Penrice, who played at QPR with Holloway as it happens. The investment in the academy is paying off. I always said I wanted players with blue in their blood – that was what I was all about – and we never had it. Most of the managers we had didn't want to look at the youth set-up as a source of players; even Jimmy had talked repeatedly about the quality of the academy but never followed that through with his team selection.

I'm more optimistic about QPR than ever now. We have the right team, the right culture, and we are starting to get the right players. It's a long-term strategy but it'll pay off.

11. The Beautiful Game

Soundtrack: *It's Like This* by Rickie Lee Jones

AirAsia has been the spine of my working life. Without it, I wouldn't have been on the starting grid at the Malaysian Grand Prix or on the Wembley pitch being lifted on Joey Barton's shoulders. But even before aviation, football had always been my passion – it's the thread running through my life.

The difference between running most other businesses and running a football business comes down to one word: control. While I can control a lot of what happens at Air-Asia, when I'm watching a football match I can't do anything. The manager picks the team and the players go out on the pitch and that's it. It's a very strange experience for me because all I can really do is cross my fingers, sit in the stand and talk to Les Ferdinand.

And you never know what you're going to get. Some days the team play unbelievably and then when you expect them to do well, they don't turn up. That's what makes it exciting and terrifying – you genuinely never know what's going to happen.

So, I'm in football because I love it. It's not a business you make money at. There are always buyers knocking on the door for QPR because a football club is a scarce asset. But I'm not selling because I love it so much.

There are lessons I have learned about football, management and leadership which I apply to my other businesses; and then, after watching football up close for five years, there are things about the game itself which I feel need to be said.

As a chairman, the first thing you have to do is to use your head all the time rather than your heart. Passion is important – you've got to have passion on the pitch – but that passion is quite different from using passion to make decisions. And I think you've always got to take a deep breath before you make a decision. Faced with a big decision, I always take a couple of days because it's too easy to react on the basis of a strong feeling.

A lot of the problems I faced early on at QPR were because I didn't question enough and I wasn't there. I thought that the people in place knew what to do and had good reasons for making the decisions they did. That's by no means always the case. It's taken me a few seasons but I now have a team that I trust running the club. This is so important because I can't be there all the time but now the decisions made when I'm away more truly reflect how I think the club should be run. On the flip side, I did learn one thing about being a leader: the necessity of focusing. When I was involved with Formula One, I was also trying to run QPR and AirAsia. None of them flourished. AirAsia in particular started to slide and that was something Din and I had built from the bottom up; I felt it should be able to continue to flourish without our exclusive attention. But it didn't. And QPR and Caterham F1 weren't working as well as they should have either. Focus, being present, watching, listening and talking to people on the ground are vital to understanding what's happening throughout a business because only that way can you

a) motivate and b) catch problems before they become infectious. To be successful you have to focus. Without that, I simply couldn't give each business the attention they needed.

I've learned that the chairman's role is agreeing on the budget, sticking to the budget and getting the right backroom staff in, and then letting them run the club. You act as a check and balance, and you see things that they don't because you're not there every day. By having the right team in place your observations should help them develop the club in the way you all want.

The board should be professionally run; the money involved in football is ridiculous so you need to take emotion out of the decisions that have to be made at that level. Then if you have a good board, a good academy, a decent squad, a decent scouting system and a good medical system, you have all the elements of a good football club. The board sets the budgets and monitors the health of the business; the academy feeds new loyal players to the squad with the club culture ingrained deep within them; the squad performs on the pitch; the scouting system brings new but appropriate players in, and by 'appropriate' I don't just mean 'successful', I mean players who have the same values and outlook as the club; and the medical staff keep the players fit and healthy. It's not a sophisticated view but simplicity is a strength. Always.

It really surprised me when I took over that the club wasn't professional in all of those respects. I didn't do anything about it – in fact, I may have made it worse – because I thought that was the way things were done. It was only after a few years that I realized it had to be run properly, like a real business. My business ideas are based on passion. I think everyone who works needs to feel passionate about the job they do. Sport, too, is all about passion and sometimes that passion can obscure the business decisions you have to make. I was guilty early on of being too passionate and of letting that cloud my judgement. The team now at QPR have the passion but are also making smart decisions for the club. Ruben and I only step in when we're needed.

I've also learned that footballers in this day and age come in two types: guys who really want to play, and guys who just take the salary and bank it. And that was something I hadn't experienced in life before QPR: a guy who was being paid £50,000 per week and still doesn't perform.

More generally, it is amazing to me that in such a big-money sport, agents are so unregulated. There should be more control and standards for agents. There are good agents out there but there are others who just destroy people's careers by putting themselves ahead of their clients' best interests. Young players can be earning a fortune without understanding anything about the real world. Their agent is often the one person they go to and trust. These agents have got to repay that trust by looking after their players properly. Regulation of agents is essential.

And I don't think clubs should pay agents, I think players should pay agents. Agents are invariably the corrupters of the game because they will influence a manager to take a player. And that's bad for the player, the manager, the club, the supporters and the game itself.

I think that the Premier League is well run at the moment. Financial Fair Play was an important step. I was actually the final vote in that decision when it was split 50/50. I think I upset a lot of the richer clubs, but I felt it was wrong for clubs to be unaccountable for their finances. Ironically, of course, QPR were done for breaking the terms of Financial Fair Play – an incorrect decision in my view, and the rules have been changed since then.

The Premier League is well run but there are a lot of problems elsewhere. There are too many games in the Championship: the league should be smaller. This fixture crush doesn't do anything for English football, yet it is an important league for the development of young English players who don't get much of a chance in the Premier League. Something has been wrong in the England team set-up for years, because when you look at the team going out to play, they look strong on paper but they never do well.

One way forward is to combine the Premier League and Championship into eastern and western leagues as they do in the US, then have a final between the winners of the leagues to decide who becomes champion. I think this would make it a more exciting season. Football, while not as bad as Formula One, has become predictable in the last twenty years. Since the Premier League started in 1992–3 only six teams have won the title – including Leicester's freakish win in 2015–16. So I think a shake-up would be good and regional leagues, followed by play-offs and then an FA Cup-style final might be interesting. These leagues wouldn't be fixed: there would be relegation from them and promotion from lower leagues so there would still be movement. This system would bridge the financial gap between Premier League and Championship clubs, which at the moment makes for an almost impossible transition. We should also add the strongest Scottish clubs into the leagues. It'd be great to have Rangers and Celtic and some of the others playing in our leagues – not that increasing the quality of the competition would help QPR but it makes sense to me to strengthen the leagues however we can. It's a pretty radical idea but I think its time has come. To my mind, it'll increase the quality of the home-grown players and the competition between teams overall.

That's a long-term plan but on a shorter time scale we need to address the fact that too many games are lost by bad decisions. And you really can't blame the referees – they're only human and the game moves at a million miles an hour, so they need all the help they can get. But the money riding on their decisions is huge. Look at rugby and cricket, which both have instant replays on key decisions. Cricket! Even the most traditional, conservative and stuffy sport has embraced new technology; it's time for football to do the same.

The live broadcasts show every decision from three different angles so the technology is definitely there. It's just the FA and the Premier League who are holding the game back. What should happen is that if the referee misses a penalty claim, an offside or a bad foul, he should be able to call on instant replay and make a decision. At least his view will be the same as the TV viewers. Sepp Blatter may have argued that it interrupts the flow of the game but, let's be honest, there are so many stoppages in football anyway that getting key decisions right is only going to improve the game. I would give teams three opportunities per game to challenge decisions and otherwise allow the referee to get on with it.

I left Warner Music because they didn't want to embrace new technology. In the same way, football is going to be damaged if the FA or FIFA don't adapt and use technology. I'd also take the Sin Bin idea from rugby. It's a fair punishment – a ten-minute sin bin wouldn't do any harm.

Finally, I have to talk about the fans. My whole life is about passion. And the passion of football fans is something remarkable. Fans get a lot of criticism because they abuse and shout at players and referees, but it's because they care so much; they love the game, they love their club and they feel every decision, defeat and victory intensely. I love that about football. Give me an example of another sport where you get 400 or 500 fans driving to Hull or Doncaster from west London on a winter mid-week night to watch their team; even if they're losing, the fans are still chanting and singing. I was looking at some posts by American sports fans; those who had been to a football match in England (and parts of Europe) couldn't believe the intensity and the atmosphere. It was unlike anything they'd ever seen in the US or anywhere else.

Football has everything: unbelievable skills, centuries-old rivalries and traditions, amazing stadiums with atmospheres that can bring tears to your eyes, a language understood throughout the world and a following whose commitment is unmatched and lasts a lifetime. Football is the best game in the world. That's why we have to protect it from being left behind.

12. Tuning Up

Soundtrack: 'We Belong Together'
by Rickie Lee Jones

The mission of the Tune Group – which is the umbrella company for my business ventures with Din – is 'To Serve the Under-Served'. That feels as relevant today as it did sixteen years ago.

We created Tune in the days when we had just acquired AirAsia; our airline has now been joined by Caterham, QPR, Mirus and a scattering of Tune-branded companies that includes Tune Hotels, Tune Talk and Tune Protect. The name came from my love of music, and the plan has always been to create a lifestyle brand with the slogan 'In Tune with Life' to complement the mission.

Din and I share a basic philosophy of trying to provide value at low cost. Each of the Tune-branded companies addresses a particular sector in that way. Underpinning this is brand extension: whether it was flying, insurance, mobile internet access or hotel rooms, the idea was that Tune would be a signpost to great value services and products. Ultimately these will be linked with a loyalty card that provides discounts and short-cuts to the things customers need.

The Tune company started with AirAsia, which I had at first wanted to call Tune Air. In our early branding discussions, we got to the stage where a designer had developed a logo and colour scheme which we started to show around.

The reactions weren't encouraging.

The minister of tourism said: 'Why would you do that? AirAsia is perfect – it gives you the sense that the airline covers the whole region and allows you a geographic identity. Tune Air means nothing.'

My former colleague at Warner Music, Kathleen Tan, was just as blunt: 'Tune Air sounds like a Chinese swear word.'

The final straw was that the staff agreed with them. While the company hadn't been great to them, they appreciated the power of the name. Din and I were persuaded.

AirAsia planes were blue. I wanted to change that and tried every colour combination I could except red. Red to me meant Virgin and there were already enough parallels and comparisons with Richard Branson for me to want to choose something different. We settled on orange and showed the pilots the designs.

'It should be red. It's your colour and it suits you. Don't worry about Richard Branson. You're your own man. Be confident.'

My own view of the comparison between me and Richard is clear, by the way. We have similar interests – planes, music, sports of all kinds – but his definition of adventure is a little different to mine. Richard's idea of a thrill is to try to cross the Atlantic in a hot-air balloon or fly to the moon; mine certainly isn't! What's the point of going to the moon? What would you do once you got there? I've got too many things I want to do on Earth to go to the moon – where there are no party places anyway. We are good friends and always try to meet up if we're in the same city, but I'm not the Asian Richard Branson as some in the media have tried to brand me. I'm very much my own man – just as the AirAsia captain put it all those years ago.

I changed the livery from blue to red and dropped the original bird device on the tail fin because I think branding is most effective when there is a single clear element: look at Nike, BP, Coca-Cola and Apple. The logo or symbol is instantly recognizable on its own, it doesn't need extra facets. So we got rid of the bird and took a simple approach which has helped make us recognizable.

The Tune logo and branding follow these ideas. A simple red logo which makes an instant impact. We've explored different products using Tune but the business I keep coming back to is Tune Hotels because I think we can make this hugely successful globally. Conceptually, it's simple: apply the AirAsia model to hotel rooms. We want to create a budget hotel that provides the basics to a high standard and make extras available at a cost. If you're staying in a city I believe that you want to have excellent internet connection, get a good night's sleep and have a good shower and then get out and explore or go to your meetings. I don't think you need a huge room, a 40-inch television, a mini-bar. Stripping down the rooms to good quality essentials will reduce the cost to the customer.

When we originally launched the idea, I admit that we implemented it poorly. We tried to charge guests for towels, soap and other standard equipment, which was both off-putting financially and way too complicated. Those problems have been addressed and, with a new management team, Tune Hotels is starting to fulfil some of its promise. There's quite a way still to go.

In theory Tune Money was another simple idea but it

has been a real struggle. I was talking recently to my great friend Jay Razak who is chairman of CIMB, and he reminded me that we fleshed out the original concept for the business on the squash court. I had always wanted to get into financial services.

We agreed that we'd start out by selling unit trusts online with the aim that eventually we'd be offering credit cards, and then develop a range of financial products. Unfortunately, the joint venture we set up drained money. It was a disaster. We continued to plough cash in, and Jay started to ask me what the hell we were doing. It was a fair-enough question: he's a banker after all and wasn't used to losing money.

I asked him to give me another eighteen months and I'd turn it around. In the end I created an insurance product and promoted it through AirAsia. It worked. Once Air-Asia was in line then we started to get business from other airlines' passengers.

My whole play was that I thought insurance was way too complicated. Have you ever read an insurance contract? If you have, you're part of a small club. Like a lot of established businesses, insurance is way too confusing for the customer. Our insurance business is profitable now but it could be so much more: the policy should be easy to understand, easy to get and easy to make a claim on; the insured period should be much more flexible and it should be possible for a group of people to club together to buy a policy if they're going on holiday together. Flexible simplicity is what I'm after – that's the kind of product I'd like to see Tune offering. Unless I'm the hands-on CEO it might not happen, but I'll keep pushing.

A couple of things have been interesting to me as lessons from the whole Tune Money venture. The first was that when I create these businesses, I initially look for expertise in the field to help and guide me. But often the CEOs I put in place actually try to emulate me and my style. When that happens they end up struggling and failing to run the company effectively. As in all things in life, you need to be your own man (or woman).

The second lesson is about disruption. It's something I come back to again and again. Whenever you move into a new market, you have to be offering something new and something disruptive. When we set up AirAsia we sought aviation industry expertise, of course, but the ones who were questioning everything, leading the company and taking on the competitors weren't from the aviation business. Din and I didn't know anything about it when we started. If you set up in a new market, employ people whose approach is to question, disrupt and create – when you hire people from within that industry, often you get people who think within the industry box; you need people who think outside it. Tune Money was led by good people but their experience was in insurance or financial services; we needed people who didn't think like they were still running old companies in those old industries.

One logistical problem with the Tune companies that we're gradually addressing is that they are separate to AirAsia. This can create conflict of interest and is in no one's best interests. In the coming years AirAsia will buy them so they are brought into the fold and the AirAsia portfolio of linked companies will be stronger for it.

So the trouble with Tune management is that, in my

view, we've never really had the right people leading. It's difficult to stress just how important selection of people is – innovation and change are critical. Businesses should be disruptive and the businesses that I've been involved with that have been successful have been disruptive. That's the model, whether it's routes or insurance.

I'm more experienced now than when Din and I started these companies and we can see how we need to do things more clearly. But, just as I don't ignore ideas from any source – email, WhatsApp message, a meeting in an airport terminal – I always want to learn new things about business and people. So I'm always up for new experiences.

13. Apprentice Adventures
Soundtrack: 'Crack That Mould' by Chris Rea

Say *The Apprentice* to someone in the US and they'll immediately think of Donald Trump. In the UK, the name will be Alan Sugar. But if you travel more widely around the world, the names will change: in fact, there are now more than twenty national versions of the popular reality TV show, with a host of different business tycoons putting wannabe entrepreneurs through their paces.

Most versions of the show, with the exception of the UK, work on the basis that each episode is sponsored by a particular brand. So each task will be brought to the series by a company which then effectively pays for the episode. Even with that the costs are pretty high – too high for most companies in the South East Asian region to fund if the programme is only aired in one country. So, instead of having *The Apprentice Thailand* or *The Apprentice Malaysia*, the producers decided to expand the format to embrace the whole of Asia – which meant in effect that the programme could potentially reach half the world's population.

However, there aren't many businesses and business leaders who are recognizable in every country. But the producers decided that I seemed to get my face out there more than most. So when they approached me, through my friends at Phar, Marcus and Nick, I was flattered.

There were a few hurdles in my mind. The first was

logistical: there wasn't space in my calendar to take time out to throw myself into the show. The second was more problematic: I wasn't sure I could do it. In much of my life, I've initially underestimated what I can achieve – whether it's to be head of house at school or to run an airline or a football club. I've wanted the challenge, but never been sure whether I could pull it off until I actually went for it.

Also, I never thought of myself as being like Donald Trump or Alan Sugar. In fact, I felt we were complete opposites in terms of both personality and approach to business. My instinct is always to give people a chance and to find a role that suits them within an organization; from what I know about them, both Trump's and Sugar's instincts seem to be that if your face doesn't fit, you're out. Added to which, I don't do the limousines, the helicopters, the bodyguards and all the trappings of the tycoon's lifestyle. Nor am I loud. People think I am, because I make a noise in the press, but as a boss I'm actually quieter. Would the show be a disappointment if I didn't act in a brash, aggressive, in-your-face style?

I resisted the approach for a while. But my publicity people at AirAsia kept telling me that it would be a huge boost for the brand, and eventually I agreed to do it. A new adventure.

The producers asked me to pick two observers who would watch the teams and report back on each task. I chose Kathleen Tan, who is smart, experienced and tough. She's a brilliant marketeer and highly social media savvy. Kat had worked with me at Warner and at AirAsia. My other pick was Mark Lankester, who I've known since primary school; he is astute, a softer character than Kat but just as insightful. I also worked with him at Warner and he now runs Tune Hotels.

The first series was intense; incredibly hard work for everyone involved, and a learning curve for me too. After Phar had managed to secure the sponsors with a little help from me, we moved to the audition stage where more than 30,000 people across Asia applied to appear in the programme. Those applications were whittled down to a hundred or so and then a final thirty. The twelve that appeared before me in the first episode were a good mix of nationalities and skill sets. I had nothing to do with them at all except for the interactions in the boardroom. Again, that was difficult for me because I love to hear people's stories and get to know them. Being aloof was unusual and I tried to make up for it in the boardroom by establishing a rapport with some of the candidates in a way that other presenters of the show had not done. You can't stop yourself being a bit of a bastard – that's the role – but it wasn't a role I particularly enjoyed.

One thing I found fascinating was how the Asian culture of taking the blame came through, especially in the early episodes. In the UK and the US, the contestants would happily stab each other in the back, trample over the bodies and present themselves confidently as the best candidate. In the first four episodes of *The Apprentice Asia*, two people fell on their swords because as team leaders they had lost the task. By Episode 4, I had to say in the boardroom, 'I don't want quitters any more,' when it looked like one of the candidates, Ningku, would put her hand up and resign rather than be fired. As it turned out,

I did fire her *because* she wanted to quit but it might not have been her had she fought her cause. As the series progressed I found it harder and harder to fire people because it became clearer how much people wanted to win.

The other key cultural difference was that the losing team leader would usually bring back the strong candidates for the final firing meeting, rather than the weaker ones. That meant I had less of a decision to make: I wasn't going to fire team members who had performed well, so I was almost always forced into a corner to choose the losing team leader. By Episode 6, I'd had enough of that and told Jonathan, the losing team leader, that I'd overrule his selections if he brought the wrong candidates back into the boardroom.

Happily for the drama of the series, the candidates got tougher and more single-minded as the episodes progressed. I don't mean they were cut-throat but they were more resilient, as you have to be when you're an entrepreneur. This was part of my reason for taking on the role in the first place. I want to encourage people across Asia to have a go at starting businesses, but to be successful, you have to be resilient, you have to pick yourself up from setbacks and find solutions when you hit problems. And you have to persevere if you believe in your dream.

There are so many people in AirAsia who started out in one role but have now found their dream by never giving up, and it's a quality I hugely admire. One story that really touched me was of Kugan Tangiisuran who from the age of eight wanted to be a pilot. His family couldn't afford the pilot courses once he left school, so he studied hospitality management and worked in hotels. In 2006 an opportunity came up at AirAsia as a despatch rider and he took it, having heard that it was a company which allowed people to move between departments.

It took Kugan eleven attempts and seven years but eventually in 2013 he passed the exams to enter the Asia Pacific Flight Training programme. He spent fifteen months studying there and then transferred to AirAsia's own flight academy for six months of intensive training. In June 2015, he qualified as a first officer. I couldn't be prouder of Kugan. At his graduation, in front of newly qualified cabin crew, pilots, engineers, ground staff and their families, I held him up as a shining example of what you can achieve if you never give up:

'There's one boy here that I got very emotional about. He dreamed of being a pilot. It took him eleven times to pass the entrance exams but he never gave up and I never allowed him to give up. I kept saying, "I don't want quitters; I want people who believe in their ability and go out there and bc the best." In my fourteen years, I've seen and heard of so many fantastic stories at AirAsia but nothing makes me prouder than to see a young man, like Kugan, who never gave up and from a despatch boy he has become a first officer. That's fantastic. I'm very, very proud of you because you've shown Malaysia, you've shown the rest of the world that with determination and never giving up, you can achieve anything. I hope all of you can take a little bit of Kugan, be your best, live your dreams and never give up.'

As I spoke I cried. His story does inspire me every day and I wanted to bring some of that insight to the *Apprentice Asia* candidates. It's too easy to give up; but if you want something, if you have a dream that won't go away, you have to keep at it.

I loved making the series. It was fascinating both from the production point of view and a personal one. I loved seeing the ambition of the candidates, the competition between them and who would win out; I was as gripped by the process as any of the viewers.

Watching the candidates develop, I think the importance of resilience, self-belief and strength of will shone through. If more entrepreneurs launch new businesses in Asia and push through the problems they encounter instead of folding, I think the series will have been worth doing. We got ratings as high as *CSI* in the end, so I hope enough people got the message.

As I write this I'm in talks for a second series. I'm keen to do it, and to help grow the region's awareness of what it takes to be an entrepreneur. As for the television side, when I finally retire, I'd love to do a talk show. Watch this space.

14. Now Everyone Can Fly
Soundtrack: 'My Way' by Calvin Harris

I've been fortunate. The dreams I stuck on my tuck box forty years ago have become my day-to-day realities.

Thirty years of determination and resilience, bouncing back from tragedy and disappointment, together with the odd slice of luck – it adds up to a life of no regrets. If I was to be run over by a bus tomorrow morning, there's not a thing I'd change: I've taken every opportunity that life has presented and made the best I could of it. If I hadn't taken Flavio Briatore seriously, I'd never have got QPR; if I'd laughed at Déj Mahoney, I'd not have had three Formula One seasons and would not be looking forward to developing Caterham Cars; and if I hadn't listened to myself when I saw Stelios on the television, I'd not have had the privilege of setting up AirAsia and working with the thousands of Allstars I see every day.

I've been rewarded, of course. Not only financially but with honours and titles from the British, French and Malaysian governments. I'm grateful and proud of the awards – even if I can't quite believe I'm worthy of them.

They are also nice to share. When I got my CBE (Commander of the British Empire) in 2011, my parents had long since gone, so I called my daughter, my mother's sister and my old school friend Charlie Hunt's mum and invited them to the investiture. As I wasn't a British national, I was supposed to get the award at the

Malaysian Embassy, but I was living in Chester Square, a fifteen-minute walk from Buckingham Palace. On 31 March 2011, I had the honour of taking my party there to receive my award. The Queen was ill so Princess Anne did the honours. I'm a republican, so it's a little hypocritical to accept these awards, but I do enjoy the ceremony – and if it brings more recognition to Malaysia and the region then it doesn't seem a bad thing.

I was made Commandeur de la Légion d'honneur in 2013 by the French goverment. François Hollande, then the French president, was in charge of the ceremony where six of us were to receive the award. As I sat there in my suit, looking around nervously, he started to read out the citation for a woman who had saved Jews from the Nazis in the Second World War, who was getting the award the same day. I sat there thinking, 'This is embarrassing – what have I done in comparison to her?' I bowed my head as he started to read out the description of my achievements. But it was incredible. He explained about how I'd changed travel in Asia, and how my work in Formula One and AirAsia had created lots of jobs for French people and provided massive amounts of work in the aviation and motor industries. I felt I could hold my head up.

What have I learned about starting and running a business? That's not a past-tense question, as I learn something every day. But when I'm asked this I often use the music business to illustrate the fundamentals of my approach. At its most basic, my philosophy is that it's all about maximizing the top line (revenue), minimizing the cost, maximizing the bottom line and having a healthy balance sheet. And for me a balance sheet is all about cash. Accountants can make the numbers appear however you like, but cash doesn't lie. Those are the financial fundamentals.

The business fundamentals boil down to four points:

1. Have a good product – whether you're selling widgets, drums or clothes, you've got to have a product people want. And it also needs to be at a price people actually want to pay, whether it's Jaguar or Proton/Hyundai, the Ritz-Carlton or Tune Hotels. If you use the music analogy, what's the most important thing? It's the song. You can have the greatest singer in the world but if it's a crap song, it's not going to get played. I always preferred to sign singer-songwriters because they could control their own destiny; if you study music history, the bands and singers that have lasted the longest write their own songs. If you have a great song with a good singer then you're made: that is your product. My product was a low-cost airline with friendly service: cheap seats to destinations no other airlines flew to, flying as many times a day as possible without frills, and not charging people for things they didn't want.

   When I tell people this, they ask about price and packaging and so on, but to me price *is* product. You're either a premium airline or you're a low-cost airline. Singapore Airlines is trying to do too many different things at the moment and that's why it's suffering. At AirAsia we have one simple message and all our effort goes into it. Having a clear message means you have a clear product which is easy to understand.

2. Once you've got a great product, you've got to let people know about it – you can have the best product in the world but if no one knows about it, you're doomed. A record company with the greatest song sung by the greatest artist is still screwed if no one knows about it. Marketing is key. So many great ideas fail because companies forget about marketing. What is marketing? Spending money on billboards, on ads, for sure, but a lot of people forget that a big piece of marketing is PR, and now that's driven by social media. Facebook gave AirAsia $150,000 to use on whatever we wanted and our team decided to spend the money on my social media accounts. At the time of writing I have 1.45 million followers on Twitter, half a million followers on Facebook and 100,000 on Instagram, which I've only just started. I reach hundreds of thousands of people every day with comments about AirAsia, QPR, Caterham and any other business I care to mention. So the benefits of PR are always underestimated. When AirAsia had no money, I was in the press the whole time, generating headlines, wearing my red baseball cap and making sure that the AirAsia brand was out there. I credit PR more than marketing for getting AirAsia where it is today, whether it's me talking to the press or a stunt like Richard and I pulled with the F1 teams.

Airlines have never spent a lot on marketing, but often when they do their messages are dumb. At AirAsia I have always focused on the price, not on fancy graphics with butterflies which tell you nothing. Why confuse the market with messages other than the one that matters? We do sometimes talk about our food but I've created secondary brands for those kinds of things. For example, the food on AirAsia is branded as Santan and we're even opening a Santan restaurant in Kuala Lumpur soon. The Wi-Fi on the planes is called roKKi and, again, we promote that as a separate brand. The advantage of this is that the AirAsia brand remains 'low fares with friendly service' while the other brands associated with AirAsia have room to create their own messages.

3. Distribution is the third element of the equation. You have to make it easy for people to buy your product once they know about it. For AirAsia, distribution was the web; distribution for music companies has evolved from CDs and cassettes in record shops to online; and one of the reasons I left Warner was because the industry just didn't get the importance of embracing this new distribution channel. The music business suffered for that arrogance.

4. The last piece of the puzzle is that you have to implement. Ideas are great, talk is cheap, but results are all that matter. Ryanair is the best company I have seen at implementing their plans.

They haven't had the constraints we've had because the market in Europe is a lot freer of government interference and control, but they are my model for certain aspects of business. (There are still things we do better – we wouldn't have been voted 'World's Best Low-Cost Airline' nine years running if we weren't doing a lot of things a lot better than Ryanair, after all!)

Implementation comes down to people and processes. So one of the things we're focused on at AirAsia is 'Ancillary', which is essentially on-board or online purchases that don't have anything to do with the flight itself or baggage: duty free, food, gifts and so on. One of the reasons AirAsia has been successful is because of simplicity and a lack of bureaucracy. As we've got bigger, the tangle of bureaucracy has grown like one of those Disney forests with sharp thorns and huge trees. Recently I've turned into the Bureaucracy Ogre, stopping more trees and thorns growing and pulling out as many as I can when I see them. Implementation has to be quick, focused, and you always need the right people to execute it. Ninety per cent of success is implementation.

Too many great ideas don't get out because the implementation isn't right. You have to move quickly because otherwise the idea dies. Of course, there can also be problems if you move too fast and you make a mistake, so there's a balance to strike. But I think quick decision-making is always better, and avoids paralysis by analysis. We've become far too spreadsheet-driven. In those early days, whether it was flight operations, ground operations or how we drove our revenue, moving fast was at the heart of AirAsia's survival.

Those are the basics of founding and creating a business, and if you lay them all down you'll succeed. Miss out on one of them and you'll fall down. At which point you have to pick yourself up and go again. Persistence and determination are underestimated virtues these days. I have seen musicians and footballers who tried to take short-cuts, but there aren't any – believe me. The greatest artists and athletes work the hardest. Short-cuts will lead to failure.

One other important lesson I've learned over the past decade is that I am seduced by talent. It's too easy to be blown away by what a football player or musician can do, the way they can make you feel when you see them perform, but that can be dangerous. You can sit back and enjoy the talent show, but don't forget that a less spectacular player who works incredibly hard is often a more valuable asset.

If you look at the growth of AirAsia, it's been about people, culture, a simple message and a brand. Through all of that it's also been about partnerships. You can have hundreds of signed contracts but if a real relationship isn't there you won't be able to grow your business.

Airlines don't exist in a vacuum. They depend on manufacturers, suppliers and financiers to get them off the ground. AirAsia is no different – part of our success is due to our long-standing partners Airbus, General Electric and Credit Suisse.

They have been with us through the good times and the bad; Airbus and GE were there when we lost millions on oil hedges and we had to take back some money we'd paid them, and Credit Suisse stuck by us when the market was short-selling our stock.

Likewise, we were there for them when they needed us. A few years ago, when Airbus introduced the option to buy one of two engines (a GE or Pratt & Whitney) with the Airbus A320neo model, no one was ordering the GE engine. I trusted GE because they have always delivered for me and now I look brilliant because GE's engine is proving to be much better than Pratt & Whitney's. When no one wanted to buy GE's LEAP-X engine, we backed it and we also helped Airbus develop and then promote the A320neo. We made sure Credit Suisse were there for every major deal we've signed and we helped them win IPO deals.

People like Airbus group chief executive Tom Enders, Airbus chief operating officer John Leahy and Jeff Immelt, who rose to become CEO and now chairman of GE, and Helman Sitohang, who is now Credit Suisse Asia Pacific chief executive, have been hugely instrumental in Air-Asia's success.

Tom Enders is responsible for transforming Airbus into the 'normal company' – to use his words – that it is today, despite its political origins. He is also an incredibly open and humble person, and helped us design the plane we wanted. John Leahy is a brilliant salesman under whose watch Airbus has significantly closed the delivery gap with Boeing. He is the man responsible for AirAsia's large order book and our continued faith in Airbus.

Jeff Immelt was instrumental in getting us the right engine deal. We couldn't get the engine deal we wanted but, by chance, he was in Asia at the time and he sent someone to sit in on discussions. After being briefed, he okayed the deal, and when his staff asked how they would report this to head office, he replied, 'I'm head office.'

Helman Sitohang is a unique banker who doesn't just look at the P&L, he values people, and it's been a pleasure to see him grow from Malaysia country manager to the most powerful man in the company's Asian region.

I've always worked hard at partnerships like these so that when problems arise we can help each other out. It's a dying concept in business, but loyalty is important in AirAsia's books. I credit a lot of my success to surrounding myself with great people like Tom, John, Jeff and Helman, and, most importantly, all of these people believe in our staff like we do. Any airline would do well having these men in their corner and they deserve as much credit as AirAsia's founders for making the dream of low-cost travel in Asia a reality.

Over time, you start to become a part of these organizations – not physically or legally, but the relationship is close. They're not just business partners, they are friends. We celebrate together and we enjoy each other's company.

Airbus is a good case in point. I first met Kiran Rao, now the executive vice president of Strategy and Marketing, in 2002. Like the meeting with Conor McCarthy at Stansted, this was not what people think of as a typical business meeting across a boardroom table. We met at the

Ben and Jerry's stand in Singapore Airport. At the time, Airbus had recognized that low-cost airlines were a potentially huge source of growth – unlike Boeing, which were still looking exclusively at the main state-sponsored airlines in the region. The meeting was brief but I think we both clicked and realized that we could do business together – which is an understatement as we're now well beyond the 600 aircraft mark with Airbus.

The negotiations with Kiran and his team are always tough but we both recognize that we're looking after our companies' bottom lines and we sign agreements that work for both of us. After that, it's party time. On one occasion in 2011, we were due to sign a big deal on a Tuesday night in a nightclub in Paris (again, we don't do boardroom deals!) and I insisted that all the senior Airbus executives, including the big man, John Leahy himself, get up and dance before I signed anything. John isn't the most natural clubber but got into the spirit of it. The reason I delayed was actually because a lot of Indians (especially from Kerala) think it is bad luck to start new ventures on a Tuesday so I made them wait till after midnight before I signed. In the meantime, it was fun to watch these businessmen on the dance floor with my cabin crew. To cap it all off, I asked the stewardesses to plant lipstick kisses on this legally binding document that would have to be presented to lawyers and I made a down payment of €20 on the multi-million-dollar deal. Once the negotiations were over, it was time to have a party!

Some people make a distinction between work colleagues and 'social' friends but I don't really see the need: I count most people I work with as friends. Of course, if there's a problem then we have to work it out, but more often than not, people I've fallen out with over the course of my career are now back as friends. When I first met Jay, we hated each other, but through working together we have a friendship that is almost a bromance. Ruben Gnanalingam has been a brilliant partner at QPR. He's been there when I really felt things weren't going the right way at QPR and we support each other. Din is more like a brother than a business partner. We're so different yet we understand each other at a level that is like family.

There have been personal sacrifices along the way. Work and my lifestyle caused my marriage to fail, a heavy price to pay. But I have put a lot of time and love into my kids and they have given me so much happiness. Over the past ten years any free personal time I had I have spent with Stephanie and Stephen. When Steph reached secondary school age, she went to Epsom College and she thrived. I missed her so much that I'd often fly to London on Friday night from Malaysia, turning up on Saturday morning to spend time with her and then returning on Sunday night. It was punishing but we had great times on those weekends. She played hockey sometimes so I'd happily go along and support her – doing what my dad never did for me, praising her when she did well.

On 25 June 2015 I drove up to Durham from my London home to watch Steph graduate from Durham University. This special day marked the end of three years in which she'd managed to balance fun with hard work – something I had never achieved. As the Vice Chancellor called her name out and it echoed through the hallowed arches of Durham Cathedral I could feel my throat tighten and I started to breathe more heavily; as she got on the stage, I let the tears flow. We still have 'hanging out' time when I'm in London now, doing the same things we did when she was at school: watching movies, going out for dinner or going shopping. Steph is making her way in the world now and we see each other as often as our schedules allow.

My son, Stephen, has had as deep an influence on me but in an entirely different way. I'm amazed at how clear he is about what he wants to do and how he wants to achieve it. He spent a year at Epsom in England before deciding he wanted to come back to Kuala Lumpur for a couple of years to experience more of Malaysia. Now he'd like to go back to England to do his A levels – and he decided and applied himself, with no influence or help from his parents. He's weighing up whether to go to university in the US, England or perhaps Japan. He has a wide view of how he can live his life and of the world.

As a twelve-year-old, Stephen got me into computer gaming. He was the one who told me we should think about artificial intelligence (AI), bitcoin and sponsoring eSports – showing me a whole new world of business potential which has also led to a wider interest in machine learning and a push for AirAsia to be data driven. I credit him with a lot of what we're doing in that field.

Although I didn't like him playing video games so much, he had a talent for it so I let that develop. In the end, he was the one who decided to stop playing them one day and moved instead to working out and improving himself physically. He taught me about self-improvement and I learned a lot from him which, as a parent, is a great feeling. I think it also proves the point that I constantly make to my staff: you can learn from anyone, at any age, so it's always worth listening. I'm forever learning new things, and I want to encourage it as a key element of our corporate culture at AirAsia.

I've been lucky to have been blessed with two children like Stephen and Steph. I also see a lot of my sister, Karena, who works at Tune Group and is close to my children. She is a constant source of inspiration to me. She got a law degree and started at the bottom but through hard work and ability has earned her place in the higher levels of the business.

I'm a social animal: although I rarely drink now, I love getting together with friends and having a laugh. Life is there to be enjoyed and you get so much more from it if you open yourself to new experiences. Music is still important; I don't get to write songs as much as I'd like to but I listen a lot to artists like Calvin Harris, Kid Ink and Pharrell Williams. You're never far away from a Steely Dan, Carole King or Rickie Lee Jones track on my playlists.

Technology excites me. Data is the new oil and, thanks to Stephen, I embrace new apps and technological innovation quickly. Over the past ten years my mobile phone has grown into an extra limb. I'm constantly in touch with my businesses, friends and staff. I love making new connections via social media because everyone has a story to tell.

The challenge of business still gets me out of bed in the morning. Whether it's Formula One or starting an airline or looking for new investments, there's always something to take on. If you don't succeed, you learn; but the important thing is to have a go.

I have no regrets but there are certainly things I could have done better – particularly at QPR and with Lotus/Caterham. Boy, did we make mistakes. In Formula One the problem was that we tried to build a team from scratch in no time at all. It's so expensive to create something as complex as a new F1 car from the drawing board in a few months, and we believed that the cost of running the team would be what we were told; it turned out to be twice as much. But the silver lining was that I met some incredible people and all my businesses have benefited from the association with the sport.

I'm fifty-three now and my life has been full. Recently I have been searching for a proper balance and I think I've got it about right. I was a man of excesses and I did everything to the max but I've come to realize that life is also about taking a break; you can't run at 100 per cent all day, every day, and die before you get to enjoy the benefits of success. You may feel invincible and that nothing can go wrong but life has a way of telling you differently: downtime is vital.

Over the past year I've learned much more about personal health (encouraged by Stephanie), because mine wasn't good at all. I am still overweight but I now understand the harmful effects of much of what we eat. Sugar is everywhere and it plays havoc with our systems. My latest drive at AirAsia is to get people to be aware of what they're putting into their bodies. And I'm taking much more care of mine. Your body is like a car: if you don't look after it, it'll deteriorate much more quickly than if you take proper care. Some people give up but it's never too late. I've had a personal trainer over the last year and I feel like a new person. Again, if I'd known before what I know now, I'd have taken things easier, but life is about balance: get work and health and relaxation in the right proportions and you'll enjoy things a lot more.

My new outlook is due in large part to a new partner in my life, Chloe, who I've been with for two years. She brings stability and she's made me reassess my life and reinvest in it.

Stephen Shrimpton, my old boss at Warner, said to me once: 'You're a typhoon, Tony. Slow down. You don't have to run at 100 mph; things will come to you.'

I feel like things *have* come to me so far. Looking ahead, transforming AirAsia to become so much more than an airline is central to my plans, as is the big push to create a genuinely South East Asian airline. I've always believed there should be an EU-style trading bloc in Asia – called ASEAN (The Association of Southeast Asian Nations). It comes from my belief in free markets: trade barriers are wrong.

It's ironic that I'm pushing for this in Asia, just as the EU is starting to fragment. Breaking up Europe is an error – it's incredibly dumb. I can see why the tensions built up: from the ruins of the Second World War, and an anxiety to stop a phenomenon like the Nazis happening again, they created a European Parliament, single currency and a vast bureaucracy that eventually strangled itself. Instead, there has to be a middle way – you can't standardize everything and there's no harm in some nationalism. The Irish will tease the English who will tease the French and so on. The single European currency was the right step from a business point of view: it's easier to trade and there's less risk. Yet it was poorly implemented – countries should have had to earn the right to be a part of it. If trade flow and GNPs (Gross

National Products) are imbalanced it causes a problem, with too many different types of economies, so I would have tiered it. If you transferred that model to the ASEAN situation, you'd have Laos and Singapore sharing a currency, which is not going to work; but one currency for Malaysia, Thailand and Indonesia could ultimately make sense.

In the early days in the music business I pushed South East Asia as a market: 'If I can sell my music to 600 million people, why not?' With AirAsia I said: 'Right, no one's looking at us yet. I'll create an ASEAN airline.' That's why we're so big, bigger than any airline in China apart from the state-owned airlines; we're number four in Asia because of our reach. I could never have created an airline with 200 planes in Malaysia alone.

South East Asia is still far from where Europe is, but we've created an ASEAN brand – perhaps the only globally recognized one – which I'm going to build on with 'One AirAsia'.

Tune is another line on my list which I need to focus on. I haven't been able to give it the energy it needs. We're trying to clean it up by putting all the related companies (Protect, Tune Talk and BigPay) into AirAsia so that the corporate governance is transparent. After we've joined everything up I'm excited about addressing Tune Hotels because the concept is so strong; meanwhile Tune Protect can become the next big digital insurance company. Each of these companies can reach their full potential once they are linked in this way.

Within AirAsia we have created something that I am proud of and hope to spend more time on: the AirAsia

Foundation. I set it up with a former AirAsia colleague, Mun Ching, in 2012.

I first met Mun Ching in 2003 when she was an online news reporter for *MalaysiaKini*. She came to see me because of my fight with the Singapore government about our route. I had got angry and the idea that the owner of a small airline would dare to take on the Singapore government intrigued her. I persuaded her to come to work for me and she led our route-planning department for four years (she'd had no experience but I could see something in her). She left to continue her studies; when she returned to Malaysia a few years later she came to see me to tell me she was setting up a social enterprise.

I was immediately on board – social enterprise has always appealed to me but I hadn't seen the right opening. It struck me that it could be part of AirAsia. We'd just been through the horror of the tsunami and the typhoon in the Philippines. Initially, Mun Ching was going to help set up a structure for an AirAsia Foundation and then launch her own social enterprise (with some funds from me). As I thought about it more, my ambitions grew. I wanted to do it properly – the tragedies that had hit the region demanded it. So we settled on a foundation that Mun Ching still runs five years later.

AirAsia provides money for grants which the Foundation gives out. I also contribute any speaking fees I get to the Foundation. And recently the commercial department at AirAsia was offered a retail space in the Klia Z terminal building which they passed on to the Foundation. The shop stocks goods from the social enterprises and any money it makes goes back into the Foundation.

The original idea was that instead of just paying out charitable givings, you take the money and try to help sustainable social enterprises. So we started giving grants and it seemed to work. A lot of the smaller social enterprises get money to start with but they don't get any help in the middle stage, so they die off after two years. Many people who support social enterprise still demand a 4 per cent or 6 per cent return on their investment. We're not about that. What we try to do is to help them grow not only by providing cash but also by helping with marketing and branding (often their plan is just to post something on Facebook, but that's not enough).

The kinds of enterprises we're helping tend to be local small-scale artisans so their exposure to modern selling techniques on social media is small. Mun Ching and her team can go in and make a real difference to a community by helping these artisans sell their products more effectively. I'm always happy to step in when I can. So when I was approached to do *The Apprentice Asia*, we organized a charity event for the Foundation which showcased some of the causes we were investing in.

The range of enterprises we invest in is expanding all the time. To date we've helped twenty, ranging from renewable energy projects to coffee collectives and tourism enterprises. Always the idea is to make an effective difference to these initiatives above and beyond a cash injection.

For example, a group of engineers who lost their jobs in the recession in Malaysia back in the nineties returned to Borneo and started working on micro-hydro turbine projects for remote villages. These places would probably never get connected to the national grid.

The engineers started innovating and installing turbines in the villages. The design process was quite basic – back-of-the-envelope sketches – so some of our AirAsia engineers went in and showed them more sophisticated engineering techniques involving AutoCAD. We have branded this the Allstars Do Good programme and encouraged our staff to take on volunteering within the Foundation – and they do a lot in their free time. AirAsia pays for their flight on a Saturday, they go out to the engineering centre and do the training.

By passing on skills and training people to provide their services using our own expertise, we can make a real difference. I love this kind of approach because it is self-sustaining – the people who learn from our engineers can pass on their new knowledge to the next group and so on.

For enterprises which make artisanal products, we look to see if we have any sales channels that might be beneficial. My dream is to create an on-board shop that sells local produce and local products; it would be incredible if we could create a sales environment where the money from sales on the plane was going back into the region rather than to huge multinationals.

The Foundation also looks after the humanitarian aid side of things. Over the years we have delivered tons of aid, transported aid workers and brought out thousands of survivors from devastated areas. As I've described earlier, we responded quickly to the tsunami crisis in Aceh and that was just the start. We were there when Nepal experienced its worst earthquake for eighty years in 2015; and we put on a huge fund-raising drive to help rebuild areas of the Philippines after Typhoon Haiyan and managed to raise over $2 million, ship in 400 tons of cargo, rebuild 532 homes and help 133 shop start-ups. It was an amazing effort. The Foundation is one social enterprise I'd certainly like to spend more time with.

When I was five, my uncle said to me that he thought one day I'd make a great politician. The comment has always stuck with me.

There's a lot still to do, though, and I want to focus more on a few projects in the next phase of my life. For example, my mind has recently been turning to two big problems. One has been prompted by my own health and the other by my experience of helping to set up Epsom College in Kuala Lumpur – the first branch of the college overseas.

If you look at airlines, they have first class, business, premium economy and economy. AirAsia only deals with economy. We leave the rest to the others. When I look at the state healthcare system, I realize they can never look after everybody satisfactorily; yet private health is beyond the means of most people, so we've got to find something in between. The way I see it is that hospitals try to do everything themselves, but 80 per cent of people probably have about 20 per cent of diseases; dealing with the 20 per cent of people who have more complicated diseases is the work of specialists, but treating them in hospitals introduces inefficiency. We should set up hospitals (Tune Hospitals perhaps) that help deal with the 80 per cent of people. If we did that, then we could be much more efficient than the state system that has to deal with all 100 per cent of illnesses, and in turn we could help relieve some of the pressures on the state.

Within hospitals themselves there are inefficiencies that

technology can iron out and we can be more flexible in the roles people perform. The health system has evolved in reaction to events from the inside. But, just as we did with the airline business, if we can come into it from the outside, we can creatively disrupt the whole network by showing a new approach and helping everyone involved, from patients through to doctors and surgeons.

Education is similar. Private education is way too expensive for most households but the state system has to be all things to all people and as a result it can't perform to the maximum for anyone. Again, if you look at the 80/20 rule, a new way would focus on getting 80 per cent of the curriculum absolutely right but provide it as an affordable private education model. I want to explore different models and try to open private education up, because in the long run it will reduce the burden on the state system.

My eye has been roving over lots of different projects and ideas recently. The focus on data, on ASEAN and the push for 'One AirAsia' are challenges that are more than enough to keep me occupied. But I am also taking a slightly longer view of things. I met up with the Formula One legend Nico Rosberg recently and we had a long conversation.

Apart from being an incredible driver and an honest, straightforward guy, there's another reason he's such an inspiration to me: he quit at the top. His view was that he'd had a dream and he'd achieved it. He could have continued to go for more goals within the sport but he decided he wanted to try other things. When he told me he was retiring from Formula One, I was really surprised because most drivers' competitive instincts force them to keep taking on new challenges. But Nico, having made it to the highest level of his sport, decided that was enough. He'd achieved what he wanted and would bow out at the top. The temptation to carry on for 'just one more year' is a self-defeating spiral.

It made me realize that great leaders know when to quit. It's an essential part of being a leader that you leave at a point when you know the company, the team or the service will improve after you're gone. I'm not suggesting that's on my horizon yet but it did make me think carefully about the future of AirAsia whenever Din and I decide the time is right.

When people recognize me in a restaurant or a club, they're shocked that I'm a humble guy: I'm not surrounded by bodyguards or weighed down by bling; in fact, I was once accused of dressing like a hobo. I don't feel the need to look smart because I think there's too much focus on appearance. Beauty comes from inside.

Having no barriers means that I will stop and chat to people – unless they just want to abuse me. I've never seen the point of retreating behind a wall because part of the reason I have been successful is that I've gone out of my way to meet and talk to people regardless of who they are. Life is much richer if you do that.

So I take the train to work in Malaysia. I get away with it a lot of the time but if one person says, 'Are you Tony Fernandes?' there's pandemonium; the whole train wants a selfie. I do that happily because it's good for me and it sets a good example to my kids.

People who don't know me and only see that I'm aggressive in the press because I fight my corner will think I'm arrogant, but I'm the same guy I was who went to Epsom

College forty years ago. I'm passionate about the things that matter to me and I'll never apologize for that.

Many CEOs and successful people believe their own press and surround themselves with sycophants who won't remind them of their roots. Again, I've never seen the point in that and I haven't let the fame and the money change me. I think it's my character, not a conscious decision, and I live by the idea that you're only as good as tomorrow. That means you can't rely on reputation or past successes to take you forward, you have continually to be better, learn from mistakes and strive to attain your dreams. Underpinning that is the belief that you should never forget where you've come from – that is a great reminder of your progress, not what people say about you or what you read in the newspapers.

If someone had told me when I was twelve that I was going to own an airline, a Formula One team and an English football club, I'd have said, 'What drugs are you taking?! Please give me some of them.' I've achieved the dreams I stuck to the tuck box, but there are still so many challenging things to do. I may succeed or I may fail. If I fail, I'll keep going until I succeed because I never give up.

That's why I'm flying high.

Acknowledgements

Writing this book has allowed me to look back and reminisce about the people who have helped shape my journey.

First of all, I am grateful to have been blessed with loving and inspiring parents who taught me compassion and instilled in me a zest for life. To my late dad, Stephen, thank you for introducing me to jazz greats, showing me the potential of supporting the underdog, and, through your dedication to public health for the public good, planting in me the desire to envision a world where equality is possible. I know we have a long way to go, but I'd like to think that whatever small steps I take to empower communities around the world are steps in the right direction.

To my late mum Ena, I owe my courage and entrepreneurial spirit. My mum's Tupperware parties were legendary, as were her skills as a hostess. She was my greatest cheerleader, always encouraging me, and she brought light and life to any room she walked into. The day she passed away was one of the darkest in my life and, till today, I cannot wrap my mind around the fact that I was not able to be with her before she passed or even fly home for her funeral, due to the exorbitant price of air travel at the time. Mum, I vowed back then that one day I would make flying affordable, and I hope that I have made you proud. Thank you for always believing in me.

Every single person I have met has taught me something. But I've been extremely fortunate to have met and worked with amazing people whom I can call both colleagues and friends. First of all, Datuk Din or 'bro' to me. (I've never understood why everyone calls you 'Datuk' and me 'Tony' – hahahaha.) Thanks for just being more than a partner-friend-brother. There isn't a word to describe our relationship. We have laughed and cried together, but always together, and always provide a backbone for each other. Thank you for coming into my life by fleecing me in the record deal for RAP. Datuk Pahamin Rajab, Conor McCarthy, Dato Abdul Aziz Bakar – without you, AirAsia would have only been a dream.

To Jay Razak aka Nazir. From enemy to besties. That's what life is all about. Many have thought we are lovers, including my daughter (hahaha). But what I have learnt about life is without friends you are poorer for it. As James Taylor and Carol King said, 'You've got a friend'. I could write a whole book about our relationship. Who knows? One day. There are many more chapters to come.

To my QPR brothers: Amit and Ruban. What a ride! Thanks for always taking the blame, for sticking together, for the laughter, the support and the words of wisdom, and for always telling it like it is. Ruban, one day we will enjoy beating Liverpool.

To Les 'Bang' Ferdinand – one day I'll beat you at table tennis or something. Thanks for being honest in this day of modern football and being the ultimate gentleman. And thanks to Ian Holloway too, for his passion and belief.

Special mention to Laressa Kelly for always putting me first and keeping me sane.

To the QPR team: let's build something special together; and to all the QPR staff: thanks for always putting the club first.

To QPR fans, thank you for standing by me and believing in the team. We're at the start of something really exciting.

To my Caterham family. Next book will be all about our new car and the making of a new Caterham. Thanks for being patient and keeping it together.

To Kian Onn and Kalli: the One-Malaysia family. We laugh and fight but you're always there for me. Without you guys, what is Tony Fernandes?

To Jeff Immelt, Mike Jones, Tom Enders, Kiran Rao and Jerome and Helman. Today business is ruthless but we have all shown that business can be about loyalty and friendship as well – we are there for each other in good and bad times.

To Martin Toseland, who captured my haphazard life and work and put it beautifully into this book: you the man; you have a gift. Admire and respect you. Sorry for being so hard to deal with!

To Jackye Chung, my tireless assistant, thank you for organising my chaotic schedule seamlessly.

To my dear sister Karena, best lawyer I know. Thanks again for always putting me first and caring about everything I do.

To Annie, who has been instrumental in everything Family Fernandes. You are the best.

I would not be where I am today without the love of my extended family of AirAsia Allstars, all 20,000 of them! Thank you for being such talented, hard-working, dedicated and creative people. It really is a privilege to lead you.

Thank you to Marcus Wright and Joel Rickett for commissioning this book, and seeing it through from idea to publication. Thank you also to Assistant Editor Lydia Yadi, as well as the copy-editors, proof-readers and the whole team at Penguin who have done a stand-up job putting my story together.

To Chloe, who has changed my life in so, so many ways; miracles do happen and you are one of the miracles in my life.

And, finally, to all the dreamers in the world. I hope this book inspires you. My message is simple: some dreams become a reality. Dare to dream.